Speaking the Unspeakable

The ethics of dual relationships in counselling and psychotherapy

Lynne Gabriel

Routledge
Taylor & Francis Group

LONDON AND NEW YORK

First published 2005 by Routledge
27 Church Road, Hove, East Sussex, BN3 2FA
Simultaneously published in the USA and Canada
by Routledge
270 Madison Avenue, New York, NY 10016

Routledge is an imprint of the Taylor & Francis Group

© 2005 Lynne Gabriel

Typeset in Times by Garfield Morgan, Rhayader, Powys
Printed and bound in Great Britain by TJ International Ltd, Padstow,
Cornwall

All rights reserved. No part of this book may be reprinted or reproduced
or utilised in any form or by any electronic, mechanical, or other means,
now known or hereafter invented, including photocopying and recording,
or in any information storage or retrieval system, without permission in
writing from the publishers.

British Library Cataloguing in Publication Data
A catalogue record for this book is available from the British Library

Library of Congress Cataloging in Publication Data
Gabriel, Lynne.
   Speaking the unspeakable : the ethics of dual relationships in
counselling and psychotherapy / Lynne Gabriel.– 1st ed.
        p. cm.
   Includes bibliographical references and index.
   ISBN 1-58391-984-8 (hardcover) – ISBN 1-58391-985-6 (pbk.)
   1. Counselor and client. 2. Counselors–Professional ethics. 3.
Psychotherapists–Professional ethics. I. Title.

BF637.C6G29 2005
158'.3–dc22

ISBN 1-58391-984-8 (hbk)
ISBN 1-58391-985-6 (pbk)

1080158
216-99

For Simon

Simon Jon Goodwin
2nd July 1974–8th November 1996

Contents

Acknowledgements

Many people have contributed to the creation and completion of this book. First, I would like to thank client and practitioner contributors for generously offering their stories of dual relationships to the original doctoral research inquiry, out of which this present book grew. The clients' and practitioners' experiences and voices form the weave of this book, but feature particularly strongly in Chapters 7, 8 and 9. I hope I have done them the justice that they deserve. My research supervisors, Dr Mary Connor and Miriam Zukas, were instrumental in my development and the decision to write this book and I am indebted to them for their integrity and commitment.

Colleagues from the Counselling Studies Department at York St John (a college of the University of Leeds) have been very supportive. In particular, I have greatly appreciated Jill Burns's incisive comments on draft chapters. Others who have read chapters include Peter Storr and Elisabeth Storrs. Their feedback has facilitated a much better book. Dr Val Wosket has been a source of encouragement from the very beginning of the venture and Lindsay Smith and Alan Dunnett have offered solace at key times. Thank you to Betty Harrison and Dr Latilla Woodburn - better grounding and support I have yet to meet! I would also like to acknowledge seminar and workshop participants whose comments have informed my thinking, as well as the many Counselling Studies students at York St John whose interest and encouragement has been touching and greatly appreciated. A special acknowledgement goes to my past and present clients and supervisees – they have richly informed my thinking and understanding of being in relationship and kept me grounded in my roots as a practitioner. Many thanks also to Joanne Forshaw, my editor at

Brunner-Routledge, who supported the project, the reviewers and their helpful comments, and the rest of the editorial team.

A very special thanks goes to my partner Pat, for her love and support and for sacrificing precious weekends in the final stages of preparing the book. Special thanks to Jean and Syd Pearson and to Darcy – the support of cherished family and friends has been vital sustenance in frustrated or dark moments.

Lynne Gabriel
July 2004

Chapter 1

Introduction and overview

This book offers a detailed and compelling story of dual and multiple role relationships in counselling and psychotherapy. It breaks new ground in offering sustained narrative on practitioner and client experiences of being in dual and multiple role relationships. At this stage, it is important to clarify what I mean by *dual relationship*. I define it here as:

> a one-to-one contracted therapy relationship between an individual in the role of 'client' and one in the role of 'therapist' which then overlaps into a non-therapy context or role. The overlapping contact occurs while there is a current therapy relationship, or before the therapy relationship is formed, or beyond its cessation. The non-therapy contact is friendship, social, sexual, collegial, financial or business oriented.

Part of the book's title – *Speaking the unspeakable* – arises directly from the accounts of client and practitioner experiences and perceptions of being in dual or multiple role relationships. In order to respect and validate their experiences, I chose to include this phrase in the title. While *the unspeakable* suggests a taboo and damaging experience, it also symbolizes beneficial and rewarding dual relationship experiences for clients and practitioners. My aim was to make the text an accessible training and practice resource that will be of value to a wide range of individuals involved in the helping professions – including practitioners, clients, trainers, supervisors and service providers.

Dual relationships are a reality for many therapists. Paradoxically, until recently, the majority of counselling texts have tended to ignore the subject, with some taking a rigid prohibitive stance

(Pope, 1985, 1988a, 1988b, 1991, 1994; Pope and Bouhoutsos, 1986; Pope and Feldman-Summers, 1992; Pope, Levensen and Schover, 1979; Pope, Tabachnick and Keith-Speigel, 1987; Pope and Vasquez, 1998; Pope and Vetter, 1991). Recent UK and USA contributions to the body of knowledge on the subject offer an alternative understanding and broaden the area to include debates on non-sexual, consensual dual relationships (Gabriel, 2001c; Lazarus and Zur, 2002; Syme, 2003).

Despite prohibitions on unorthodox contact between therapist and patient, historically, eminent practitioners did engage in non-therapy contact with their patients. Jung, Ferenczi and Rank had sexual relationships with their patients (Mann, 2001), Freud regularly met his patients outside the confines of the analytical space and Klein analysed her own children (Masson, 1985). In recent years, Thorne (1987) disclosed his willingness to extend the usual parameters of the client–therapist work and relationship into sexual dimension and contexts. His disclosure sparked a furious row within the profession and led to bitter wranglings and swift reactions from professional bodies through increasing prohibitive codes of ethics and practice (for example, BAC, 1998).

Given the diversity and complexity of contemporary social, cultural and professional contexts, the power and prevalence of a dual relationship taboo might seem a bizarre phenomenon. For instance, there are increasing cases of clients and their therapists encountering one another in numerous non-sexual contexts. Of key significance in any opposition to dual relationships is the association they have with *sexual* relationships between clients and their therapist. However, this emphasis ignores the domain of *non-sexual* dual relationships between clients and their current or former therapist. For instance, there are many examples of clients and their therapists successfully living and working in the same locale (Gabriel, 2001c; Gabriel and Davies, 2000; Lazarus and Zur, 2002). There is little published material about this type of relationship, yet assumptions abound about the potential for harm. Significantly, aside from literature by clients about their experience of therapy (see, for example, Heyward, 1993; Sands, 2000, 2002), we know relatively little about the *client's* perspective on client–therapist relationships.

In view of the extent of opposition to dual relationships and the lack of pragmatic texts and resources, the prospects for naïve or inexperienced practitioners who encounter them is likely to be poor. Consequences for clients in dual relationships with ineffective or *unintentionally* abusive practitioners are probably grim. The consequences for clients in relationships with *intentionally* abusive practitioners are bleak. Paradoxically, the potential for the practitioner to be harmed in a dual relationship is rarely considered. If dual relationships were on a spectrum that ranged from *unacceptable* to *acceptable* and their current status was firmly located at the 'unacceptable' end, I sense we are about to witness a shift towards the *acceptable* end and see a concurrent increase in texts on non-sexual, non-abusive relationships. With this in mind then, a key aim here is to offer insight into and understanding of *harmful* and *helpful* dual relationships and broaden the debate on ethical duality and diversity in helping relationships.

The book's conception

My interest in dual relationships grew from a small-scale qualitative project I conducted in the early 1990s as part of an MEd. in counselling (Gabriel, 1996). On that occasion, I researched therapists' experiences of boundaries in lesbian therapist–lesbian client relationships. Findings revealed that most were concerned about how to manage therapy relationships that overlapped into non-therapy contact and contexts. Throughout the early and mid-1990s I also personally experienced a number of overlapping social and professional contacts with former and current clients. Looking for resources to help me deal with these situations, I discovered that few supportive or advisory texts were available. Dual relationship literature at that time was virtually non-existent in the UK, although some texts and articles existed in the US field. Paradoxically, however, there seemed to be an unspoken convention, condoning those relationships that did occur. Essentially, it was a case of learning through trial and error how best to respond to the relational issues that arose. Fortunately, I had good supervision, as well as several colleagues who had experience of dealing with dual relationships and were willing to discuss and share 'good practice'.

My curiosity led me to want to hear from others who had engaged in a dual relationship, to find out how they had dealt with these relationships and to discover what could be learned from their experiences. The lack of pragmatic and accessible material for clients and therapists currently in a dual relationship, for those contemplating entering one, those who anticipate or expect to be in one, or anyone wanting to explore them at a conceptual and theoretical level, is problematic. However, recent publications in the UK and USA (Lazarus and Zur, 2002; Syme, 2003) have gone some way to redress this.

My research, practice and writing are informed and influenced by a range of philosophies and theories. My core practitioner training was based on humanistic psychology. Although I have no formal psychodynamic training, I spent several years in psychodynamic therapy and supervision and draw on psychodynamic thinking to inform my helping work. In recent years, I have been increasingly drawn towards social constructionist ideas and welcome a view of the world that embraces diversity and difference, recognizes multiple realities and acknowledges the role our social history and context play in human experience and perception.

In addition to the personal and professional influences outlined above, there are other professional matters that impact on the existence and timing of this text. In particular, I refer to the rapidly developing identity of the counselling and psychotherapy field. In relation to the status and identity of 'counselling' and 'psychotherapy' as a unified helping 'profession' within the UK, it is likely that a more corporate and cohesive identity will arise through the anticipated compulsory regulation and registration for counselling and psychotherapy practitioners. However, the categories and clauses of a system for regulating practitioners and their services have yet to evolve. Nevertheless, despite the uncertainty around the future of compulsory regulation, or questions about a cohesive identity for counselling and psychotherapy, principles of ethical practice and a degree of professional status and identity already exist, promoted by the codes of ethics and practice and the registration schemes of professional organizations such as the British Association for Counselling and Psychotherapy (BACP) and the United Kingdom Council for Psychotherapy (UKCP). For ease of reference, I refer to 'the counselling and psychotherapy field' as 'the profession'.

Overview of the chapters

Key areas covered across the chapters include:

- the complex, multidimensional nature of dual and multiple role relationships;

- client and practitioner experiences of being in dual or multiple role relationships;
- client and therapist thinking on how to/how not to respond in different roles;
- client and therapist capacity to sustain self in complex relational situations;
- relational intimacy in client–therapist relationships;
- the individual's intentionality in the relationship;
- the notion of the client's and therapist's relational responsibilities;
- the idea of forming a relational ethic for helping work and relationships.

In Chapter 2, I examine attitudes towards and beliefs about dual relationships. First, I construct a working definition of 'dual relationship', then go on to briefly discuss dual relationship classifications and consider questions of relationship type, including whether they are intentional or unintentional. I note several conflicts and confusions about dual relationship status and identity that are conveyed by the question, 'just what is a dual relationship?' Chapter 3 addresses the taboo on dual relationships and shows how prohibitions on sexual dual relationships have influenced attitudes towards all non-sexual and non-therapy relations between clients and therapists (here the terms 'client' and 'therapist' refer to individuals either currently or previously in the roles of client and therapist). Issues of whether, and how, to break the taboo on speaking out about dual relationships are considered. I examine claims about the harmful nature of dual relationships between clients and their therapists and review evidence on the type of damage that can occur. I consider relevant US and UK theoretical and empirical work, discuss how it informs dual relationship conventions, attitudes and practices and suggest that traditional psychotherapy theory is invoked to support prohibition, rather than used to critically conceptualize or pragmatically inform the complex relational situations that are likely to arise in dual relationships. In Chapter 4, I consider non-sexual dual relationships and dominant discourses that influence our thinking about these relationships.

In Chapter 5, I discuss specific opposition to client–therapist dual relationships that is based on the belief that dual relationships create role and boundary problems. To inform the discussions, I draw on concepts and insights from a number of psychosocial and relational approaches to therapy, including humanistic, psychodynamic and role theory. Chapter 6 identifies and examines significant ethical and moral dimensions of dual relationships, including professional beliefs, expectations and ethics in relation to client autonomy, therapist fidelity and relational integrity.

Ideas and developments from biomedical and nursing ethics (Beauchamp and Childress, 1994; Parker, 1991; Sim, 1997), feminist critiques and representations of ethics (Chase, 1996; Gilligan, 1982; Koehn, 1998; Sherwin, 2001), as well as narrative-informed ethics (Almond, 1998; Josselson, 1996; Widdershoven and Smits, 1996) inform my discussions. I consider principles, virtues and rights in the context of relational issues that are thought to occur in dual relationships. Client and practitioner experiences of dual relationships are represented in Chapters 7, 8 and 9. Chapter 7 provides an overview, while Chapters 8 and 9 give detailed client and practitioner experiences of being in dual and multiple role relationships. In Chapter 10, I posit a relational ethic for dual relationships and Chapter 11 concludes the text.

While the book represents a comprehensive review of the issues of dual relationships in counselling and psychotherapy, it nevertheless is a partial representation, set as it is against the contemporary UK counselling and psychotherapy field and informed by contributions from the literature and research. I offer it as a thought-provoking contribution that will stimulate further debates.

Although I have chosen to define terms used infrequently in the text in the context in which they arise, commonly used terms are clarified here. Throughout, the pronouns 'she' and 'he' are used as and where appropriate. The terms 'counselling' and 'counsellor', as well as 'psychotherapy' and 'psychotherapist', are used at various points. Usually the inclusive terms 'therapy' and 'therapist' or 'practitioner' are substituted.

This terminology does not aim to exclude particular theoretical orientations, practices or practitioners, but instead seeks to move away from any divisive stance associated with disagreements and divergent thinking about these professional titles. The terms used here represent those who identify as counsellors who counsel their clients, those who identify as psychotherapists who engage in psychotherapy, as well as those who lay claim to both.

Chapter 2

Dual and multiple role relationships in counselling and psychotherapy

we need to come to terms with the fact that some of the psychotherapeutic profession is in a state of denial around dual relationships, role confusion and the inadvertent and unintentional interpenetration of role boundaries.

(Clarkson, 1994: 37)

WHAT DO WE MEAN BY THE TERM DUAL RELATIONSHIP?

Attitudes have not changed much in the years since Clarkson (1994) argued that the therapy profession was in a state of denial and confusion about dual relationships. Many of us might continue to be uncertain about what we actually mean by the term *dual relationship*. Interpreting it is a helpful starting point. According to the British Association for Counselling and Psychotherapy (BACP, 2002), dual relationships 'arise when the practitioner has two or more kinds of relationship concurrently with a client, for example, client and trainee, friend and client, colleague and supervisee'. On the other hand, the British Psychological Society (BPS) have regarded dual relationships as those 'in which individuals engage in a personal loving and/or sexual relationship with someone to whom they also have professional responsibilities' (BPS, 1997: 36) as well as those 'in which the psychologist is acting in at least one other role besides a professional one' (BPS, 1997: 39).

For example, a dual relationship exists where a client and her/his therapist also share supervisee and supervisor contact. It exists where a client–therapist relationship (a current or previous relationship) develops into an intimate and loving friendship or a sexual relationship. This raises questions regarding what constitutes sexual and non-sexual dual relationships; an area that until recently received little attention (Gabriel, 2001c; Gabriel and Davies, 2000; Lazarus and Zur, 2002; Syme, 2003). How might we distinguish between the qualities or characteristics of a sexual or a non-sexual dual relationship? A sexual dual relationship could appear relatively simple to identify, whereas a non-sexual one might seem a more complex phenomenon to interpret. Pope and Vasquez (1998) believe that non-sexual dual relationships occur when:

> the therapist is in another, significantly different relationship with one of his or her patients. Most commonly, the second role is social, financial, or professional. In some cases, one relationship follows the other. The mere fact that the two roles are apparently sequential rather than clearly concurrent does not, in and of itself, mean that the two relationships do not constitute a dual relationship.
>
> (1998: 190–1)

We can also distinguish between non-therapy and therapy contact, as in Gabriel's (2001c) definition, suggesting that a dual relationship occurs when:

> a one-to-one contracted therapy relationship between an individual in the role of 'client' and one in the role of 'therapist' overlaps into a non-therapy context or role. The overlapping contact occurs whilst there is a current therapy relationship, or before the therapy relationship is formed, or beyond its cessation. The non-therapy contact might be friendship, social, sexual, collegial, financial or business oriented.
>
> (Gabriel, 2001c)

A wide-ranging definition of dual relationship phenomena is offered by Lazarus and Zur (2002: xxvii) who suggest that these relationships are 'virtually any association outside the "boundaries" of the standard client–therapist relationship – for example, lunching, socializing, bartering, errand-running, or mutual business transactions (other than the fee-for-service)'.

What is absent from these definitions is the notion of *intentionality*. Whether a relationship is intentional (that is a reasoned and consenting participation) or circumstantial (that is brought about by chance) is probably a significant factor in how a client and therapist respond. If there is mutually agreed intent to extend the therapist–client relationship into personal or social roles, then the outcome might differ radically from a situation where a predatory practitioner has intentionally (sexually or psychologically) exploited a client.

Not only can we consider the ways in which we interpret the term 'dual relationship' and their intentional or circumstantial nature, we also can think about the circumstances in which the relationships arise. Pearson and Piazza (1997) offer this useful index:

- **circumstantial multiple roles:** coincidental meetings, such as brief, unplanned contact at shops or other social contexts;
- **structured multiple professional roles:** prevalent in counsellor education and supervision where trainers and supervisors may hold multiple roles, including teacher, advisor, mentor, supervisor;
- **shifts in professional roles:** such as a change or shift in organizational structure that changes relationships of those in the organization;
- **personal and professional role conflicts:** a preexisting professional relationship is followed by a personal relationship, or conversely, a personal relationship precedes a professional one and,
- **the predatory professional:** an abusive professional who deliberately seduces or exploits their clients, unconcerned with anything but their own needs.

This is a helpful, although limited index. It offers useful explanatory terms, but excludes features that are likely to be significant in dual and multiple role relationships, including the cultural context of the individuals involved in the relationship or overlapping contact. By *overlapping contact* I mean, for example, the type of circumstantial contact referred to by Pearson and Piazza, or situations where the individuals live and work in rural or minority communities (Gabriel and Davies, 2000).

DUAL AND MULTIPLE ROLE RELATIONSHIPS: TABOO OR TO BE?

In attempting to define and interpret dual relationship, we can see that the definitions suggest there is a sanctity and 'sacredness' inherent in both thinking about and being in a client–therapist relationship. The overlapping of this sanctified professional helping relationship into areas regarded as taboo or abusive, such as a sexual dual relationship between client and therapist, suggests a parallel with incestuous relationships. Parker makes the point that an incest taboo 'functions importantly in boundary maintenance and identity formation, without which a cultural mode of life is not possible' (Parker, 1976: 299) and encourages an individual's participation in wider networks of relationships in order to form a differentiated concept of self in relation to others. In the context of a dual relationship, we might question whether the therapist or the client can differentiate between the roles of the relationship, as well as wonder how they will cope with transitions across dual or multiple roles, from therapy to other types of contact and setting. Clearly, this is complex relational terrain.

Deeming what is acceptable or taboo occurs not only through our legislative systems, but also through cultural, social and professional customs and mores. Definitions of taboo reflect this and suggest the degree of power that exists in something deemed 'taboo': 'the system or act of setting a person or thing apart as sacred or accursed; a prohibition or restriction imposed by social custom . . . to put under a taboo; to exclude or prohibit by authority or social influence' (*Oxford Reference Dictionary*, 1986). Within counselling and psychotherapy, codes of ethics embody and promote this idea in portraying the sacrosanct nature of the client's status in the therapy relationship and the need to protect their interests by prohibiting certain therapist actions. For example, BACP states that:

> [P]ractitioners must not abuse their client's trust in order to gain sexual, emotional, financial or any other kind of personal advantage. Sexual relations with clients are prohibited. 'Sexual relations' include intercourse, any other type of sexual activity or sexualized behaviour.
>
> (BACP, 2002: 7)

With regard to dual relationships, BACP states that:

> [T]he existence of a dual relationship with a client is seldom neutral and can have a powerful beneficial or detrimental impact that may not always be easily foreseeable. For these

reasons practitioners are required to consider the implications of entering into dual relationships with clients, to avoid entering into relationships that are likely to be detrimental to clients, and to be readily accountable to clients and colleagues for any dual relationships that occur.

(BACP, 2002: 5)

These statements make it clear that sexual relations with current clients are prohibited and that *any* relationships, including potential or actual sexual relationships, with former clients require caution and critical consideration. The implicit message, that some therapists might intentionally or unintentionally exploit their clients, is contentious as well as disturbing in a profession that promotes a duty of care to clients and prizes fitness to practise of its practitioners. What is more, in situations where the client and therapist enter some form of 'taboo' relationship, perceived expectations of therapist competency and capacity to care for their clients can lead to self-censorship and withholding of information in supervisory contexts (Bond, 1997).

A therapist's theoretical orientation might also contribute to a dual relationship taboo. For example, a psychodynamic or psychoanalytical informed approach is more likely to advise against dual relationships, on the premise that they interfere with the development and progression of the transference relationship: a key feature of analytically oriented therapy. However, the roots of the contemporary taboo probably lie much earlier than current theory. In the early twentieth century, Freud drew on a number of sources including anthropology, mythology and biology to develop his concept that the human animal is driven by instinctual sexual and aggressive drives (Freud, 1962). These drives were controlled through socially and culturally defined processes, experienced in a community context and sublimated through engaging in socially acceptable activities. Such activity would contain unacceptable behaviour by repressing original drives through subscription to socially sanctioned prohibitions such as the widespread taboos on incest and sexual exploitation of children. According to Browne (1984), we construct taboos in complex ways and in the process swing between polarities of 'right' and 'wrong':

Throughout human experience the pendulum of attitudes and behavior has swung back and forth between the extremes, depending largely on basic and primitive impulses. As people have felt secure the pendulum has been inclined to hover on the positive side, with the light, the happy, the free. Contrariwise, as people have been individually or collectively insecure, lonely, threatened, they have tended to drive the pendulum to the negative, dark side of existence and to emphasize the forbidden . . . there can be comfort, or pretended comfort . . . in the things one cannot do.

(Browne, 1984: 1)

Here, Browne highlights a number of features that might operate in a dual relationship taboo. Clearly, he conveys a process of thinking and behaving that is subject to change over time, as well as psychological processes or constructs such as security and insecurity, ambiguity, fear or defensiveness. These might equate with how people think and act in dual relationships. For instance, dual relationships could be associated with the 'dark side', or forbidden side of client–therapist relationships, and linked with taboo sexual relationships. A sex-oriented taboo could operate in any relationship where it is imagined that the potential exists for sexual contact to occur. Obviously, the relative privacy and anonymity of a one-to-one therapy relationship invites comparison. Clarkson notes that 'the incest taboo in psychotherapy is clearly important because of the intense intimacy of the counselling/psychotherapy relationship' (Clarkson, 1995: 24). Dualistic notions of right and wrong behaviour in the therapy relationship have probably led to dual relationships being split off into a mass-prohibited category. Clarkson also notes the paradoxical and dual nature of many phenomena in human living, including notions of black/white, good/evil and life/death. This paradox probably exists in our struggles to deal with ambiguity and intimacy in living and relating.

Self-concept and professional identity will also feature in and influence ways in which we construe or respond in complex relationship situations. For example, a practitioner's need to have their supervisor regard them as effective might prevent them disclosing their ambiguities and challenges in a dual relationship they have developed. Practitioners tend not to discuss personal and professional anxieties since it can render them vulnerable, challenging the profession's (and the professional's) perceived image of competency and reliability (Bond, 1997). Sadly, this line of thinking can induce a sense of shame whenever the practitioner experiences confusion or uncertainly, or makes an error of judgement. According to Kaufman and Raphael (1984), awareness of this process can trigger a further sense of shame which then sets in motion a vicious circle, with the practitioner continuing to withhold their feelings of shame for fear of being seen as incompetent or inferior. A sense of shame can induce feelings of being 'bad', associated with fear of other people's negative reactions (Parker and Schwartz, 2002). According to Parker and Schwartz (2002), the negative or bad aspects of a situation and the person's core self can become equated so strongly that they become the same, to the degree that in shame 'the self is pictured as unable to cope, and as an object of scorn, contempt, ridicule, disgust, or rejection' (Parker and Schwartz, 2002: 312).

Worryingly, if shame generates silence, this suggests that dual and multiple role relationships remain unexamined with peers, colleagues or supervisory consultants, thus the taboo continues. Especially problematic are situations where the practitioner's understanding of the relationship occurs at the 'edges of their awareness' (Wosket, 1999; Mearns, 2003). From here, decisions or actions about the relationship may take place without a deeper understanding of underlying motives or presuppositions. Clearly, the idea of publicly identifying as, or with, a 'wounded healer' who is psychologically unavailable to the client (Sedgwick, 1994) or may inflict harm on them, is likely to be unappealing for the majority of practitioners. Thus, the taboo and its associated silence prevail.

REALISM IN RELATION TO DUAL RELATIONSHIPS

We cannot ignore the fact that dual relationships occur. Those who acknowledge that these relationships are unavoidable are often involved in situations of complex social, cultural or occupational diversity. Consequently, when a dual relationship occurs, the therapist and client have to find ways to deal with it, rather than abolish or deny it, or manage it 'in secret' (Clarkson, 1994, 1995; Clarkson and Murdin, 1996; Gabriel, 2001c; Gabriel and Davies, 2000; Syme, 2003; Wosket, 1999). Others are even more positive and proactive in their thinking about dual relationships. For instance, Tudor (1999) suggests that the capacity to move between various relationship roles promotes equality and mutuality and provides the opportunity to deal with, rather than avoid, relational complexity, while Lazarus and Zur's recent US text offers a range of rhetorical and anecdotal support for dual relationships (Lazarus and Zur, 2002). In addition, taking supportive attitudes towards dual relationships into a human rights context, Welfel (1998: 169) argues, 'repudiating all dual relationships is inconsistent with the right to free association that citizens in a democratic society have'.

Generally, however, we tend to base arguments for dual relationships on personal rhetoric and experience rather than empirical research findings. Consequently, not only do the prevalent discourses and conventions deny the existence and potential positive possibilities of dual relationships, but also we find that arguments in support of these relationships receive less recognition and credibility within the helping profession. The force of dominant arguments against dual relationships has until recently silenced a more liberal ethic. Yet, its presence opens up the possibility, as well as the reality, that some people, in some contexts, do experience successful dual relationships. While those who speak out in support of dual relationships are few in number (see, for example, Clarkson, 1994; Gabriel and Davies, 2000; Hedges, 1997; Lazarus and Zur, 2002; Syme, 2003; Tudor, 1999), nevertheless, their existence provides a critical counterpoint to a historically dominant prohibitive ethic. Characteristic of these approaches is the recognition and acknowledgement of multiple, diverse contexts and the need to be 'fluent' across a number of roles. Rather than deny duality and complexity, liberal approaches raise the possibility that it is less likely to be the relationship itself that is problematic and more often than not the way the therapist handles the dual relationship.

Those with a tolerant attitude to dual relationships appear to share a willingness to acknowledge diverse and complex social contexts, as well as an awareness of the practical difficulties involved in ethically managing dual or multiple roles. Implicit in their arguments is a case for identifying pragmatic and ethical solutions as part of a morally defensible dual relationship ethic. However, Pope and Vasquez (1998) would counter this approach with an assertion that it constitutes a defensive strategy in order to field criticism of dual relationships. While counterpoints and challenges of the nature of Pope and Vasquez's provide helpful reminders of the ethical enormity of a dual relationship, they might be punitive.

For instance, what does their line of thinking say about human nature? It seems to imply a distrustful stance and the idea that therapists cannot be trusted. Nevertheless, such suspicion might be met by further defensive attitudes on the part of practitioners and elicit yet more counter-challenges. There is an inherently 'stuck' quality about this pattern of interaction. What might be more productive is a willingness to consider alternative perspectives and solutions to dealing with duality and dual relationships. If therapists are willing to explore their concerns and dilemmas about dual relationships in a non-defensive and educative way, offer healthy challenge to dominant thinking, as well as to one another's practices and theories, then maybe there is a greater chance of learning how best to manage concerns and issues. This opens the possibility for an exploratory dialogue within the literature and helping practice that is counter to what Hedges terms naïve moralizing (Hedges, 1997: 221). According to Hedges, uncritical assumptions serve only to foreclose on critical and open debate. Moreover, he believes that a 'dual relationship witch-hunt' prevails (Hedges, 1997: 221). Clarkson (1995) echoes this assertion with her claim that the profession is phobic and defensive about dual relationships and 'witch-hunts' rather than that it identifies ways to deal with these relationships. Given that we are not in Salem and that our aim is to expand and develop our knowledge and practice in ethically aware and appropriate ways, it is time for changed approaches to thinking about the complex reality of dual relationships.

As noted, some therapy approaches appear to be more positive and proactive in their attempts to identify ways of working with complex relational matters (Mearns and Thorne, 2000; Rowan and Cooper, 1999; van Deurzen, 1998). For example, from a person-centred position, Mearns and Thorne (2000) promote the idea of inner psychological configurations of the self as a way of understanding the multifaceted nature of the person and their relational style with self and others. Although the idea of the configured self is not new (Horowitz (1988), for example, interprets it from a psychodynamic perspective), Mearns and Thorne's person-centred conceptualization is a helpful way to think about our multiple internal representations and self in relation to being with self, others and our surroundings.

In order to rebut critics of the person-centred practitioner's willingness to face the complexity of work with loose boundaries in therapy relationships they state that:

The willingness of person-centred therapists to extend sessions, increase frequency of sessions, allow telephone contact, engage in home visits, and respond to client requests for mild physical contact like a hug, are all so manifestly inappropriate within other theoretical models that they are automatically taken as evidence of *over-involvement*. It is fascinating that ethical challenges are made on the basis of over-involvement, yet there are no codes which describe a pattern of systematic therapist *under-involvement*.

(Mearns and Thorne, 2000: 50; original emphasis retained)

Clearly, the authors take issue with their differently oriented critics and infer that the objective, distant stance characteristic of under-involvement, which they infer to be psychodynamically oriented approaches, is inappropriate in their experience and vision of a therapeutic relationship. Mearns (1997) also posits the idea of 'full involvement', where the therapist faces the challenge of offering congruent and empathic relational depth in the client–therapist relationship. Additionally, Mearns offers an important distinction between 'over-involvement' and 'full-involvement'. In the latter, the therapist makes clear professional decisions that fully account for the client and therapist's relational boundaries. Involving his or her supervisor in the process of monitoring full-involvement is a sign of the therapist's capacity to manage the relational depth. Alternatively, in over-involvement, the therapist crosses relational boundaries for his or her own gain, usually unwilling or unable to use supervisory support to monitor the process. Mearns and Thorne's concepts resemble Sarbin and Allen's (1968) notions of role enactment and the capacity of the person to achieve optimal relational distance that avoids under-distance or over-distance. Moreover, as Landy (1996) points out, a concept of 'distancing' is useful since its helps a client to find:

a balanced psychic position between an overdistanced [*sic*] stage of repression and an underdistanced [*sic*] state of emotional flooding, so that catharsis may occur, thus helping the individual restore psychic equilibrium and move toward an understanding of his therapeutic dilemma.

(Landy, 1996: 32)

Consistent with Mearns and Thorne's (2000) work is the idea of being literate in ethical and relational matters (Gabriel, 2001b) in order to achieve a 'good enough' relational stance. In keeping with this notion, it is possible to imagine a dual relationship situation where the therapist is able to maintain a good enough attempt at full involvement in the therapy relationship, while attending to the relational conditions and requirements in the overlapping contact with the client. Proactively dealing with this duality and multiplicity will be demanding. The client and practitioner dual relationship experiences shown in Chapters 7, 8 and 9 suggest that the capacity to be aware of 'self' and 'other' and to be able to distinguish these states is a critical ability for the therapist in a dual relationship. It is conceivable that a therapist might be either unable or unwilling to support the client to achieve this optimal position. Clearly, it is a demanding position for the therapist and asks a lot of their skills, knowledge and experience, as well as their capacity to 'hold' all the relationship roles in an ethically sound way. Then again, a therapist might not have developed sufficient competence or confidence, so feel unable to deal with the situation. Therapists are human, thus fallible. While there may be no shame in acknowledging this fallibility, paradoxically, it is harmful to deny it or be silent.

The dominant taboo status of dual relationships continues to silence therapists, and clients, who experience them, while the predominant reports on harmful emotional and psychological effects on clients are likely to result in the silence continuing. Arguably, however, remaining silent is surely an implausible option for counselling and psychotherapy – a profession that expressly aims to support clients to find healing narratives or strategies for dealing with life and relationship problems.

Without a doubt, the novice therapist enters difficult relational territory when attempting to negotiate dual or multiple role relationships, manage the boundaries between various and diverse relationship roles and deal with relational ambivalence and ambiguity. As such, we need to identify resources that are conceptually and clinically helpful, across a range of contexts. For example, on some occasions, person-centred theory might offer appropriate tools through which to review the client's locus of evaluation in the dual relationship and the power balance in their various roles, while at other times, psychodynamic theory may provide useful insights into relational dynamics between client and therapist. Given the potential contexts, types of relationship and people involved, any one of a number of theoretical approaches could apply. Relationships are as a constellation of fluid and interactive events with intrinsic influences and features that both hinder and facilitate (Lewin, 1948), therefore it would be naïve and idealistic if we seek a template for successful relationships. After all, as humans, we constantly run the gamut of relational joy and angst. While there is no shame in acknowledging our fallibility, paradoxically, it might be harmful to deny it through being silent.

SILENT WITNESSES

Being silent about dual relationship experiences denies opportunity for healthy challenge and inhibits publication of helpful literature on this type of relationship. Tudor (1999) suggests that professional silence and lack of literature occurs because dual relationships are a 'hot potato'. As a means of dealing with 'enforced' silence, a practitioner or their colleagues can effectively 'split off' the fact that a dual relationship exists (Pope and Vasquez, 1998). In these situations, individuals enter into a tacit agreement to ignore their own or other's ethical violations. This type of defensive reaction resembles the psychoanalytical notion of 'splitting' (Cashdan, 1988), whereby unwanted material (for example, thoughts or information) is literally split off as a form of psychological 'protection'. A taboo on disclosing difficult dual relationship material could operate in a supervisory context. For example, a less experienced therapist might be unable to manage the degree of relational intimacy that can develop in long-term psychotherapeutic work and might find it hard to disclose their struggles with or feelings towards the client to their supervisor (Webb, 2000). Where, then, does that leave the practitioner? In all likelihood, they will be silent, as well as unsupported or unchallenged in their relationship with the client. If the supervisee/therapist is silent, then the dual relationship remains unexamined.

While dual relationships that are intentionally sexually, psychologically or financially abusive are inexcusable and therefore rightfully taboo, unintentional abuse arising, say, from a therapist's ineptitude or inexperience, is likely to be indefensible in the context of litigation. As a result, we should not be too surprised that the prospect of disclosing information about being in a dual relationship, or about a colleague who is in a dual relationship with a client, can be problematic. For example, inhibition about disclosure might be associated with the professional prohibition on sex between therapists and their clients. A practitioner might link this prohibition with any kind of sexual or intimate contact or content. For instance, one manifestation of this could be the denial of their sexual feelings towards clients. In an anonymous survey of US psychologists, Pope and Tabachnick (1993) found that of 400 respondents, 87.3 per cent admitted to feeling sexually attracted to a client. Yet, many therapists are unable or unwilling to openly disclose or discuss their sexual feelings with peers or supervisors (Corey, Corey and Callanan, 1993). Non-defensive discussions of therapist attraction to clients are rare, but do appear in the professional literature (see, for example, Webb, 2000; Wosket, 1999) and suggest shifting attitudes on what constitutes unorthodox material for publication and debate.

Evidence to support the notion that practitioners encounter problems speaking out about contentious or taboo topics exists in Lindsay and Clarkson's (1999) survey research into practice incidents that practitioners found ethically troubling. They surveyed practitioners (1,000) registered with the United Kingdom Council for Psychotherapy (UKCP) and received 213 replies, of which 12 per cent expressed concerns about dual relationships. Practitioners are more likely to talk about their own and their colleagues' dual relationships when professional conditions, including those encountered in a training, supervisory or some other learning and development context, are conducive to discussing dual relationship questions, concerns or issues in a non-defensive, non-accusatory way.

There are compelling reasons for breaking the dual relationship taboo and speaking previously unspoken details about dual relationships. Breaking silence will advance our understanding of complex relational situations and bring debate of these into a public domain. Significantly, open and transparent debate is likely to encourage a less fearful culture in which discourse need undergo less personal and professional censorship. However, there are signs that it is becoming more acceptable to acknowledge personal vulnerability and psychological wounds. For example, the idea of the therapist's 'shadow side' (that which is regarded as the darker side of a person's character; their negative personality or behavioural traits) is an increasingly common topic (Page, 1999; Wosket, 1999).

THE CLIENT–PRACTITIONER RELATIONSHIP

The relationship between client and practitioner implicitly weaves its way throughout this book. Obviously, in a client–practitioner dual or multiple role relationship, at some point a therapy dimension will be a feature of it. Without a doubt, theoretical perspectives and preferences will influence the practitioner's views and practices in the relationship. The centrality of the relationship is given more weight in some therapy approaches, such as psychodynamic and person-centred, but less so in others, such as cognitive-behaviour therapy. From a person-centred perspective, periods of uncertainty are characteristic of the work and relationship and the self of the therapist and their way of being in the relationship is a key therapeutic 'tool'. Questions about therapist capacity to provide core relational qualities such as empathy, congruence and positive regard, as well as weather the vagaries of relating and working through relational ambiguity, are central. A clear sense and understanding of self is both necessary and significant. Alternatively, from a psychoanalytical position, traditionally, the practitioner maintained a more distant stance with the aim of securing an uncontaminated frame for the relationship (Langs, 2004). A move into unorthodox territory, such as a dual relationship, 'contaminates' the client–practitioner transference relationship and impedes clinical interventions and interpretations.

We know little about individual capacity to sustain self in the face of complex dual relationships and even less about relational processes that inspire and allow mutuality and negotiation of roles and responsibilities. Until recently, the Western European helping field has largely focused on an individualistic notion of self in therapy theory, practice and relationships. Critical inquiry and interest in narrative and social constructionist approaches to helping work and relationships is increasing (see, for example, Angus and McLeod, 2004; Etherington, 2000; Gergen and Kaye, 1992; McLeod, 1997; McNamee and Gergen, 1992; White and Epston, 1992; Winslade and Monk, 1999) and broadening the resources available to us.

Ideas about relating across different relational dimensions, as would be the case in a dual relationship, already exist in counselling and psychotherapy theory. From an analytical perspective, Greenson (1967), conceptualized the reality (the here and now

'real' relationship) and fantasy dimensions (the transference relationship) of the relationship between client and therapist. Building
on these ideas, Bordin (1979; 1994) saw the relationship as a
'working alliance' with a characteristic three-fold dynamic: (a)
bonds (the emotional bond between client and therapist); (b) goals
(the overarching aim and purpose of the therapy); and (c) tasks
(the interventions required to reach the goal). Central to Bordin's
concept is the belief that this frame can guide the therapy work, as
well as become transferable to other types of helping relationships
(Bordin, 1979, 1994; Horvath, 1994; Horvath and Greenberg,
1994). More recent interpretive and psychodynamic conceptions of
multiplicity within helping relationships, including some which
embrace social constructionist and postmodern influences, can be
found in an edited text from Rowan and Cooper (1999).

Despite a widespread belief in the significance of the therapy
relationship, it is important to question any uncritical assumptions
that the relationship between client and therapist is central to the
entire therapeutic enterprise (Feltham, 2000a). As noted above,
our concepts of self, self in relationship and self in context are
changing. In addition, our knowledge continues to develop on the
qualities and effectiveness of the relationship between practitioner
and client (Feltham, 2000a, 2000b; Horvath, 1994; Horvath and
Greenberg, 1994). Then again, questions about the relationship will
continue to remain unanswered as therapy continues to evolve in
the face of wider social, cultural and political forces. On the other
hand, we do know a lot about one aspect of client–practitioner
relating – when clients and their practitioners enter into sexual
relationships. We turn now to consider these.

Chapter 3

Sexual dual relationships

> It is generally agreed that sexual boundary violations remain harmful to clients no matter how much time elapses after termination of therapy.
>
> (Corey *et al.*, 2003: 277)

CLIENT–PRACTITIONER SEXUAL DUAL RELATIONSHIPS

Undoubtedly, the most taboo of all client–practitioner dual relationships are those of a sexual nature. The profession regards a sexual relationship between a client and their therapist as an exploitative use of the therapist's power, role and status in the relationship. It is widely believed that they cause considerable psychological harm to the client (Pope and Vasquez, 1998). Furthermore, some equate sex between a client and therapist with incest or sexual abuse (see, for example, Gabbard, 1989; Pope, 1988a). A characteristic feature of any 'abusive' sexual relationship is the violation of a client's rights, in tandem with the therapist's abuse and exploitation of their power in one or more of the dual relationship roles.

If we look at the structure of the word *therapist,* we can construct *the/rapist.* While this might seem a powerful indictment of a professional role, nevertheless, it acknowledges the potential for abuse of power within the role of therapist. The term 'abuse' is cited in the professional literature, yet rarely defined. Given that arguments against dual relationships presuppose some form of client abuse, as practitioners it is important to clarify the meaning of the term. As Russell points out, 'sexual abuse has become a blanket term which in fact can refer to a myriad of experiences and behaviours' (Russell, 1993: 2).

Ethics codes are unanimous in their prohibition of sex between client and practitioner. However, ambiguity continues about what constitutes problematic sexual contact and, as Russell points out, sex and sexuality are complex constructs that will be influenced by our societal context and ways in which we see the world (Russell, 1993). Bond (2000) suggests three types of sexual contact are problematic in a therapy relationship:

- **sexual assault** (deliberate and forceful attempt to have some sexual contact);
- **sexual abuse** (some manipulative pressure to enter into sexual contact under the guise that it will be helpful to the client); and
- **sexual harassment** (where the therapist makes deliberate physical contact, gestures or comments that are not welcomed by the client, or are expressed through an unequal power dynamic in the relationship).

While Bond cautions against harmful sexual activity, he also comments that there can be positive and life-enhancing connotations to sexual activity which are associated with intimacy and physicality, although these are usually located outside the therapy relationship in friendship and social relationships (Bond, 2000). Coleman and Schaefer (1986) point out that the type of abuse experienced by the client can range from 'the psychological type', where the therapist satisfies their emotional needs through the client, to 'covert sexual' behaviour, such as hugs or sexual gazes and, finally, to 'overt sexual' behaviour, including sexual intercourse.

Explorations of erotic feelings between client and practitioner are not commonplace in the literature, yet we are expected to be alert to the forms of seduction that play out in the therapy relationship (Orbach, 1999). According to Mann psychoanalytic theory and practice has:

> evolved in order to deal with the passions of the erotic transference and countertransference. Almost all the techniques of psychotherapy have their origin in an attempt to defuse the

possibilities of the therapist and patient developing a sexual relationship.

(2001: 63)

He sees the unconscious as essentially erotic in nature, providing motivation for our individual needs for others (Mann, 2001). In relation to client–therapist relating, if a client presents with sexual abuse issues, the therapist and client's unconscious erotic communication could become difficult. As such, therapist and client need to work towards a state of 'good enough incestuous desire' (Mann, 1999), which involves acknowledgement of eroticism and recognition that it will not be acted upon in the relationship. Then again, this recognition presupposes the practitioner will uphold psychoanalytical ideas on eroticism, yet as noted earlier, erotic feelings in the client–practitioner relationship rarely feature outside analytical theory. Unless training curricula include eroticism, at present, few other resources are available to practitioners.

Even more ambiguous is the position on sexual contact between individuals whose therapy contact has ended, although a recent US survey on post-termination sexual relationships found that these relationships can be harmful (Pope and Vetter, 1991). According to Thoreson, Shaughnessy and Frazier (1995: 88): 'counsellors need to be able to differentiate between sexual attraction, which is inevitable, and sexual acting out, which is unethical and destructive'. Nonetheless, those who imagine it is 'safer' to enter into a sexual relationship with their client beyond the ending of the therapy relationship might be alarmed by the findings of US research. From a survey of 958 clients who had been sexually involved with their therapist after termination of the therapy, 866 reported that they had experienced harm as a result of the relationship (Pope and Vetter, 1991). A striking feature of the findings is the number of clients (32 per cent) who had experienced an earlier incestuous or sexually abusive relationship. Table 3.1 summarizes the clients' characteristics.

It appears that the damaging consequences are far-reaching and include ambivalence, guilt, or impaired ability to trust, as well as confusion about roles and boundaries. Complaints and reports of abusive dual relationships received by POPAN (Prevention of Professional Abuse Network) are certainly testament to these findings. While statistics show 32 cases of sexual abuse of clients by therapists between 1998 and 1999 (POPAN, 1999), POPAN claims

Table 3.1   Characteristics of clients (n=958) who have been sexually involved with a therapist

Characteristic	N	%
The client was a minor at the time of the involvement	47	5
The client married the therapist	37	3
They had experienced incest or other child sex abuse	309	32
They experienced rape prior to sexual involvement with the therapist	92	10
They required hospitalization, considered to be at least partially due to the sexual involvment with the therapist	105	11
They attempted suicide	134	14
They committed suicide	7	1
They achieved complete recovery from any harmful effects of sexual involvement	143	17
They were seen pro bono or for a reduced fee	187	20
The client filed a formal complaint against therapist	112	12

Source: summarized from Pope and Vetter (1991).

this is likely to be a significant understatement of the problem. A profile of abuse cases for 1998–9 shows that a significant percentage (total 35 per cent) of alleged abusers were either counsellors or psychotherapists (POPAN, 1999). However, organizations like POPAN will only attract those who are aware of its existence or are able to disclose their story of an abusive relationship with a helping professional, therefore figures are unlikely to accurately portray the extent of practitioner sexual abuse. Importantly, it is unlikely that every aggrieved or abused client will be able, or inclined, to express their experience of abusive therapy (Heyward, 1993; Sands, 2000).

A study of women sexually exploited in therapy found that a high proportion of exploitation occurred while they were working to resolve previous sexual abuse (Russell, 1993). Russell (1993) identified a range of harmful effects of the abuse, including: feeling special in the relationship; feeling dependent on the therapist; having trust in the therapist and the relationship betrayed; guilt feelings, especially in relation to betraying the therapist if they disclose information about the relationship; feelings of anger; feeling frustrated or/and helpless; ambivalence; poor or distorted self-concept; feeling isolated; feeling desperate or suicidal; and problems in subsequent therapy.

Russell's findings suggest that ambivalent feelings about the therapist and the relationship could trap a client in a confused and/or painful state. According to one participant:

[I]t's taken me a long time to make any sense of it, because people who did know about it . . . used to make it out to be a really big scandal or be really horrified, and I couldn't relate to that . . . I wanted them to understand and they didn't. Many years later, looking back on it and seeing it from a feminist perspective, I'm supposed to see it that I've been sexually abused and maybe that is the case but I can't put it into that mould either, because I always felt that I'd been very much part of it. I'd never been a kind of innocent victim.

(Russell, 1993: 27–8)

While, on one level, this client appears to be saying that she played a willing part in the sexual relationship, on another, there are questions about how she was induced to participate and what role her earlier experiences played in her responses. Perhaps an unscrupulous therapist might take advantage of this.

Some of Russell's participants spoke of the atmosphere of concealment that shrouded the sexual relationships and many of them felt trapped in a web of secrecy and conflicting feelings (Russell, 1993: 41). She quotes at length one participant whose experiences embody the feelings of many of the clients. It is worth including a considerable portion of the quote, since it outlines some of the damaging relational dynamics that can occur, and, in particular, shows how clients can blame themselves:

I am still struggling with the guilt at ending the sexual side of the relationship. At some level or another, it feels like abandoning a needy, helpless child who doesn't understand, and is totally bereft . . . I also recently talked with a friend with whom it transpired my therapist had a sexualized relationship as well . . . hearing her describe all the feelings and conflicts I have had, including the guilt, protectiveness, and saying how persuasive she had experienced him as being. Although mostly I desperately wanted and needed the relationship, at the times I didn't want it, or didn't want to be sexual, I was totally unable to say no . . . I felt paralyzed . . . I have despised myself for letting him use me all those times.

(Russell, 1993: 41)

Russell also addressed the part that therapists play in exploitative boundary transgressions, drawing largely from client narratives and informing her discussion with anecdotal evidence from informal discussions with therapists. Client impressions of the therapist included beliefs that the therapist was needy, feelings that the therapist was unable to handle the relationship or a sense that they were lacking in proper training and supervision. Russell's findings about client experiences and perceptions of being sexually exploited by their therapist are consistent with US research and writing on sexual contact between clients and therapists. For example, Pope (1988a) outlined the following similar wide-ranging and damaging cognitive, emotional and behavioural consequences for the client of having sexual contact with their therapist:

- **Ambivalence** in the client's feelings towards the therapist; uncertainty about whether their experiences should be disclosed; can involve the client treating the therapist as a parental/ authority figure; one the one hand client may feel rage, but on the other hand may experience separation anxiety;
- **Guilt feelings**; feeling that it is their fault;
- **Feeling empty**;
- **Feeling isolated**;
- **Sexual confusion**; for example, the therapist sexualizes a client's request for physical comfort;
- **Impaired ability to trust**; where the client's trust is betrayed, they are reluctant to invest further trust in the therapist;
- **Ambivalent role identity and role reversal**; the client can feel responsible for the therapist's feelings and actions, becoming a therapist to the therapist;
- **Emotional lability**; the tendency to feel strong, varied emotion in inappropriate contexts;
- **Suppressed rage;**
- **Cognitive dysfunction;** including, for example, inability to concentrate, preoccupation with what has happened, and flashbacks;
- **Increased suicide risk** resulting from the abuse experience.

The emotional, psychological and relational consequences of sexual relationships between a client and their therapist are clearly far-reaching. Pope (1988a) argues that professionals must be aware of the impact on a client of entering a sexual dual relationship with their therapist:

[A]wareness of the scope and nature of the damage caused by sexual contact with clients is important to all of us as professionals. Such awareness can help each of us as individuals to avoid any temptation to act out sexual attraction to a client, can prompt us as a profession to create and implement *effective* measures to ensure that clients are protected from such abuse and from exploitive therapists.

(Pope, 1988a; original emphasis retained)

Few would argue with the sentiments of client protection and safety expressed here by Pope. They lend support to arguments that 'counsellors need to be able to differentiate between sexual attraction, which is inevitable, and sexual acting out, which is unethical and destructive' (Thoreson *et al.*, 1995: 88) and support claims that clients need to be provided with information about what is acceptable or unacceptable therapist behaviour (Thorne, Shealy and Briggs, 1993). The following example suggests one such case:

Mary is a tutor on a Diploma in Counselling course at a university. She also works in private practice as a counsellor and also a supervisor to a number of counsellors in the area. One of her supervisees, James, asks for advice about a situation he is in. James says that he finished therapy with his counsellor some three months ago, after seeing her for almost two years. He felt therapy had been really good and he had really liked his therapist – and recalls having experienced some quite strong feelings of sexual attraction towards her. Recently they met by accident whilst out shopping and his therapist invited him to meet her for a drink in a week's time, which James accepted. His therapist is a very experienced counsellor and supervisor and also occasionally teaches some one off sessions on the Diploma course.

What if . . . James keeps the appointment?
What if . . . James and his former counsellor become friends?
What if. . . they enter into a sexual relationship?
What if . . . James decides he wants to see his counsellor again for therapy?

(*Source*: Gabriel and Casemore, 2003)

On the other hand, we need to guard against the defensive pendulum swinging too far towards the prohibitive end, with the result that the therapy environment loses sight of humane concerns (Lazarus, 2001; Greenspan, 1993). Lazarus suggests that fear of lawsuits or complaint action causes many therapists to practise in a 'bizarre and dehumanizing way' (Lazarus, 2001: 2). From fear of litigation or complaint, the therapist adopts a defensive and distant stance. Arguable, this strips the relationship of spontaneous and genuine relating and is surely anathema to approaches that see the relationship as the medium of change.

As noted earlier, client–therapist sexual relationships have been likened to incest and rape (Gabbard, 1989; Pope, 1988a). Pope (1988a) suggests that the psychological impact of sex with one's therapist can remain latent, only to be triggered by some later emotional experience. A therapist's intentional abuse or accidental mismanagement of the therapy boundaries might resonate with a client's earlier abusive experiences and interfere with the process of therapy. An individual client's, or therapist's, capacity to form differentiated relationships and deal with complex boundary issues will correspond with their ability to manage a dual relationship. Evidence suggests that relational problems are especially confused and complicated where the therapist also has encountered past sexual abuse (Pope and Feldman-Summers, 1992). Where this is the case, closeness in the client–practitioner relationship might be confused with sexual intimacy.

INTIMACY BETWEEN CLIENT AND PRACTITIONER

Although *sexual* intimacy is widely regarded as inappropriate in the therapy context, some approaches, such as person-centred therapy, value *emotional* intimacy between client and therapist. There seems to be a fine line between what is deemed acceptable or unacceptable, manageable or unmanageable and appropriate or inappropriate intimacy between a client and their therapist. A classic case of sexual and emotional intimacy between therapist and client was Thorne's public disclosure about sexual encounters with a female client (Thorne, 1987) in what he argues was appropriate action with that particular client, at that particular time. In an interview with Windy Dryden (Dryden, 1987) two years before publication of this experience, Thorne spoke of the importance of 'different kinds of boundaries' in a way that perhaps foreshadowed his later sexual encounter. He described relationships with his clients that on occasions might extend to sharing a meal, yet also spoke of his apprehension about 'moving into a minefield' and described the thinking process that informed his actions:

> am I really saying to some of my clients: 'I am not just willing for you to be my client, I am actually willing for you, in a significant way, to become part of my life? Which isn't necessarily to say I am willing for you to become one of my intimate friends, although it might mean that eventually. However, I am willing for you to occupy more space in my existence than simply the therapeutic hour'. If I am saying that then where, as you say, does the limit actually come? All I can say at the moment is that I am trying to be open to that question without getting too worried about it.
>
> (Thorne, quoted in Dryden, 1987: 53)

In the same interview, Thorne raised the question: 'if you profess that person-centred therapy is essentially about attitudes and a way of being, what distinguishes your behaviour in the therapeutic session from your behaviour outside of it?' (Dryden, 1987: 51) and argued that, for some clients, it could be beneficial to meet outside the context of the traditional therapy hour. Not only that, it might be immensely enriching for both client and therapist. Essentially, the client could learn how to give through, for example, inviting the therapist to meet socially. When asked whether the client would be able to understand the expanded therapist role, Thorne responded:

> I think that would depend almost entirely on the way in which my relationship with the client was being negotiated. I would certainly wish to ensure that as we explored the extension of the traditional therapeutic boundaries, some of the potential pitfalls are looked at in advance. Indeed, in the work that I have already done in this direction this has certainly happened. In other words, if it seems likely that an extension of the role outside the therapeutic hour is desirable and we explore the possibility of doing that, at the same time, we will begin to look at some of its implications, both before the event and

after it. So, certainly, what I am saying is that I would expect both myself and my client to monitor very closely the effects that this extension of role was having on the two of us.

(Thorne, quoted in Dryden, 1987: 57)

In his response, Thorne communicates a close attention to the process and detail of the relationship and appears to consider and value the client's understanding and experience of what happens in the relationship. He speaks of monitoring and discussing relationship changes, as well as tracking their impact. While it is likely that some psychoanalytic or psychodynamic therapists threw up their hands in horror at Thorne's sexual behaviour with a client, equally, Thorne might argue that he attended to the ethical detail of the relationship and sought client consent to participate. Thorne seems to have mutually negotiated meaningful and intimate connections in a congruent, transparent way. According to Langs (1982), we dread meaningful relatedness because it can lead to the unfolding of primitive and psychotic fantasies and perceptions. Perhaps Thorne was not afraid to approach a deeply meaningful way of relating with his client. Although it is unlikely that Thorne's account is unique, in the years since his public disclosure of sexual intimacy between himself and a woman client, the professional climate has become increasingly intolerant of such actions and disclosures. Thorne's case raises questions about a client's capacity to freely participate in and monitor a changing relationship. How can we be sure that a client is able to enter into what seems to the therapist to be a mutually negotiated relationship?

This is a tricky topic and recent research points to its complexity. In relation to how clients behave towards their therapists in the therapy relationship, Rennie (1994a, 1994b, 1994c) identifies what he terms 'client deference' and believes to be a major property of the client's perception of the relationship with the therapist. When discussing the concept of deference, Rennie points out that:

> *[D]eference* is commonly defined as the submission to the acknowledged superior claims, skill, judgement, and so forth of another person. In the therapy dyad, the therapist is generally considered to be more expert than the client – a situation that could be expected to potentiate the client's deference to the therapist.
>
> (Rennie, 1994a: 428; original emphasis retained)

He also notes that the client's covert processes remain unspoken, as a preferred deferential strategy. Clearly, a therapist might interpret this silence as assent. Alarmingly, when thinking about how a client might behave in a dual relationship, Rennie's work suggests that they might defer to their therapist by, for instance, sensing that the therapist's intervention is inappropriate or inaccurate, but nevertheless, remaining silent in order to avoid challenging. Not only might the client defer to the therapist's requests or interventions, they could also become confused about what constitutes abusive therapist behaviour (Finkelhor, 1986). Rennie suggests that using *metacommunication*, or 'communication about communication' (Rennie, 2001: 87) in the therapy practice and relationship helps to overcome unhelpful deferential dynamics and can reduce misunderstanding in the communication between therapist and client. Rennie makes the point that when the therapist invites the client to comment on what they have said or done 'it is a bid to access the unspoken' (Rennie, 2001: 87).

Clearly, intimacy between client and therapist is a complex and potentially problematic area of therapeutic relating – possibly because of associations with sexual intimacy, or concerns about appropriate/inappropriate client–therapist relational proximity. What seemed to be the essence of Thorne's justification for sexual intimacy with his client was the notion of paying scrupulous attention to the ethics and moral integrity of the situation (McCartney, 1966). Since then, attitudes towards sexual intimacy between helper and client have become increasingly prohibitive. Thorne's (1987) account of sexual intimacy with his client was published nearly two decades ago. McCartney's (1966) promotion of 'ethical sex' and the use of therapists as surrogate sexual partners with clients appeared in the 1960s when sex therapy often literally meant sex with clients. The use of surrogate partners in sex therapy was common in the US and UK (Cole, 1988), although, as Cole points out, this practice was rarely discussed in the literature and was increasingly criticised as unethical and inappropriate treatment (Cole, 1988). The intervening years since have seen considerable change in attitudes and a growing emphasis on a policy of no sex between helper and client.

Crucially, however, the client's account is missing from the literature noted in this section. For some of the client participants in this study, it was evident that an intimate bond with their therapist was a significant feature of the relationship. We need to be open to the possibility of misconstruing intimacy as 'pseudo'-closeness (Russell, 1999: 197), whereby we go through the motions and offer the pretence of relational closeness. From the experience of those client participants who had a damaging experience (as represented in Chapter 8), it would seem that there was no genuine intimacy in the relationship. That said, achieving 'healthy' intimacy or relational depth might not be a straightforward matter in close relationships. According to Holmes (2001), the paradox of intimacy is that we can only be achieve it if we can negotiate separateness successfully. Those with difficulty in separating out from a significant relationship may find intimacy hard to achieve. For some individuals, in some contexts, intimacy that overlaps into non-therapy contexts may be inadvisable.

Mearns narrates the powerful story of being in a session with a client, Terry, and shares the client's reflections on being in a helping relationship with him:

> All the way through the session I was filled with such a wide range of emotions – it felt like I was exploding. Watching that on the video, it doesn't really come across. Another thing was that it felt like Dave was doing an enormous amount right through the session. Again, when watching the video he seems to be very quiet and there were a lot of silences. But 'silences' isn't a word that I would use. It felt like – at points it was unbearable, the amount of emotion and the intensity of the interaction between the two of us.
>
> (Mearns, 2003: 7)

Meeting the client at relational depth can have an intensity that borders on the passionate and spiritual. Mearns uses the term 'relational depth' as secular language to describe powerful relational phenomena (Mearns and Thorne, 2000: 56). In his later years, Rogers noted his awareness of the mystical quality of working at relational depth and commented that 'I am compelled to believe that I, like many others, have underestimated the importance of this mystical spiritual dimension' (Rogers, 1980: 130). More recently, in relation to work with one of his clients, West (2004: 174) reports similar inexplicable shared phenomena that felt like 'we were that closely, that deeply engaged in exploring the topic, in a way akin to Buber's I/Thou relating'.

This mystical relating is a powerful experience influenced by qualities that may transcend the limits of our present understanding (Clarkson, 2002). Navigating our way through appropriate relational depth and avoiding over-involvement in the client–therapist relationship will probably require a deep understanding of self and self in relation. We might also come face-to-face with the paradox that our most private places are also those that we wish to share (Mearns and Thorne, 2000). With the depth, intensity and mystery of I–Thou relating (Buber, 1937), we will constantly tread the edges of our awareness. Perhaps it is stating the obvious to say that this demands an intensely aware and reflexive way of being in relation to self and others, as well as the courage to navigate the perimeter of our relational understanding. Undoubtedly, an appropriate baseline for practice is 'no sex with current clients' since there is no logic of justification for sex with clients, but equally, from the discussions above on I–Thou relating, there is evidence to support non-sexual therapeutic intimacy.

Chapter 4

Non-sexual dual or multiple role relationships

non-sexual dual relationships, while unethical and harmful per se, foster sexual dual relationships.

(Pope, 1990: 688)

To assert that self-disclosure, a hug, a home visit, or accepting a gift is likely to lead to sex is like saying doctors' visits cause death because most people see a doctor before they die.

(Zur, 2002a: 47)

NON-SEXUAL CLIENT–PRACTITIONER CONTACT

Examples of one-to-one therapy relationships that extend into other contexts and types of client–practitioner duality exist in some therapy approaches. For example, in cognitive-behavioural therapy (CBT), contracted therapeutic work can involve contact between therapist and client outside the context and confines of the consulting room. A therapist might accompany the client who, for instance, is fearful of supermarket queues, to do their shopping with the aim of supporting them to overcome their fears. The therapist regards the non-consulting room contact as a task-focused, contracted activity. Essentially, the therapy relationship and work extends beyond the 'frame' (Gray, 1994) of the traditional therapy hour and consulting room context into a wider helping arena.

From a transactional analysis (TA) approach, Tudor (1999) notes that until recently it was commonplace for a TA trainee and trainer to also relate to one another in a client–therapist relationship. According to Tudor, many TA therapists left BACP in the 1990s because of BACP's prohibitive stand on client–therapist and concurrent trainer–trainee roles. Yet ironically TA therapists' professional body, the Institute for Transactional Analysis (ITA, 1998), now advises against this type of dual role and prohibits combining the roles of therapist and supervisor. The TA approach also combines the role of one-to-one therapist with group facilitator, so that a client might engage with their therapist in both individual and group therapy contexts. Essentially, the therapy boundaries extend from client–therapist relating into facilitator–group member contact.

This practice of extending the therapy space is not unique to TA, however. From a psychodynamic approach, Holmes (2001), working from an attachment-informed perspective, suggests that clients who relate with a disorganized attachment style (that is, where the experience of being cared for was traumatic, such as in cases of sexual abuse) will possibly shift between very different ways of being. This might require the therapist to adopt a range of strategies, including writing, telephoning and visiting the client until the relationship or therapeutic alliance is strong enough for them to feel some sense of security (Holmes, 2001).

Other examples of extended therapy and therapeutic boundaries include a therapeutic community, where it is common for workers to hold multiple roles and a worker may counsel a community member as well as share the same living and social space as the member (Kennard, 1998). Furthermore, in a pastoral context it is common for the pastor to provide religious ministry as well as spiritual guidance and community fellowship (Krebs, 1980; Montgomery and DeBell, 1997). What seems central to the approaches noted is a *well-intentioned* extension of the therapy boundaries, to create an extended therapeutic space in which the individuals remain in the roles of client and therapist.

NON-SEXUAL, NON-THERAPY CONTACT

While most practitioners and professional bodies agree that sexual relationships with current clients are potentially abusive or damaging and that sex with past clients should be avoided, there is no such consensus on the legitimacy or otherwise of entering into non-sexual dual relationships.

According to Pope and Vasquez (1998: 193), there are several significant reasons why a non-sexual dual relationship is problematic, thus taboo. First, a client can experience psychological harm from their dual relationship partner's power, status and control over them (I use the term *dual relationship partner* here to denote either individual in the dual relationship). The power differentials in the client and practitioner therapy relationship complicate matters and impact on the client's status in the relationship. Therefore, the client cannot be an equal partner in any secondary relationship role(s). A second reason is the belief that secondary roles erode and distort the therapy relationship and generate conflicts of interest, which in turn compromise a therapist's capacity for sound professional judgement. A third reason to avoid non-sexual dual relationships is because they interfere with the beneficial impact of therapy that continues beyond termination of the therapy relationship. Finally, if dual relationships were acceptable, clients and therapists would behave differently and some therapists might screen clients for potential friendship or business relationships. In Pope and Vasquez's view, practitioners offer a range of self-gratifying or specious justifications for being in non-sexual dual relationships. These are summarized in Table 4.1.

Others have objected to non-sexual dual relationships on the grounds of a correlation between sexual and non-sexual dual relationships. According to some critics, a gradual erosion of role boundaries in a non-sexual dual relationship culminates in a sex-based relationship (Borys and Pope, 1989; Edelwich and Brodsky 1991; Schoener, 1999). Over time, then, the relational boundaries erode and the line between appropriate therapy contact (that is, the contracted therapy work) and inappropriate contact (such as deepening intimacy with increasingly sexualized contact) blurs, fostering sexual relating (Pope, 1990). Edelwich and Brodsky (1991) note that most cases of sexual misconduct begin with minor boundary violations such as inappropriate self-disclosure by the therapist, touching the client in a non-sexual way, or seeing the client socially. In a similar vein Coleman and Schaefer (1986) suggest that abuse can occur across a continuum of psychological and sexual intimacy between client and therapist and that problems arise when the therapist sets poorly defined boundaries.

While it is possible for there to be a causal link between such boundary 'violations' and the development of a sexual dual relationship, there appear to be unexamined assumptions that

Table 4.1   Ways in which professionals justify non-sexual dual relationships

Justification	Example
Selective inattention	The dual relationship is made tolerable by the therapist blocking out awareness of the relationship, splitting the two relationships and refusing to acknowledge that both involve the same client and have implications for the client and their therapy.
Benefits	The therapist claims that the dual relationship is beneficial for the client and could produce effective therapetic change.
Prevalence	The therapist claims that many others enter into dual relationships, therefore they are legitimate.
Tradition	The therapist claims that the dual relationship is created through an exchange of services and that this type of bartering relationship is traditional.
Client autonomy	The therapist believes that the client wanted and chose the relationship.
Necessity	The therapist claims that the relationship was unavoidable.

Source: summarized from Pope and Vasquez (1998: 199–206).

therapists cannot, or will not, manage the boundaries of the relationship. A central feature here seems to be therapist integrity. There seem to be assumptions here that therapists who enter dual relationships do not possess this quality. While this uncompromising position leaves no possibility for any beneficial affects from being in non-sexual dual relationships, it does suggest a vigilant approach that might be missing in some therapist training and supervision. Notwithstanding the intentionally abusive or exploitative therapist, it is feasible to assume that some therapists either do not know how to deal with the relationship or underestimate the potential dangers of a non-sexual relationship. There are surely major implications here for providers of counselling and psychotherapy training and supervision. Proponents of a more liberal view of dual relationships, Lazarus and Zur (2002), argue against Pope and advocate a permissive stance that is relevant to the client–therapist setting and relationship, as well as the practitioner's theoretical and clinical position. They suggest that overlaps between therapy and social, friendship or business can work and claim that arguments against non-sexual dual relationships because they harm a client, are unproven and erroneous. That said, consider Sally's case, which although hypothetical, is an amalgam of actual events.

What if . . . client and practitioner live in the same town?

Sally is a newly qualified counsellor who lives and works in the same small town as many of her clients. She often encounters them at shared social and recreational venues, or in contexts such as the local GP's or dentist's waiting room. Sally works part-time as a counsellor in the local GP surgery, as well as a few hours a week counselling in a local secondary school, and she now wants to develop a small private practice. Sally values her social life and does not want either herself or her partner to miss events and activities that they enjoy. For example, they both are keen bowlers and Sally often sees current and former clients at the local bowling club. She feels uncomfortable about the reactions of some of her clients when they meet in these overlapping contexts. Currently, a few of her new clients appear to be either embarrassed about seeing her in contexts outside the therapy room or want to spend time in her company. In addition, some of the school clients that she works with want to seek Sally out when they meet in social settings and often want to introduce her to their friends and family. She feels unsure about this. As she was between supervisors for a short while (she decided to change supervisors at the end of her training period) she discusses the situation with a couple of her course colleagues and an experienced counsellor colleague who works in an organisation providing staff counselling. Each of them told her they thought she was being unprofessional and unethical and should stop seeing her clients and work in other contexts, away from her town.

(*Source*: adapted from Gabriel and Casemore, 2003)

The scenario above, shows a dangerously naïve way of conducting dual or multiple role relating. As suggested in the story, Sally is a newly qualified practitioner, which might account for some of her naïvety. On the other hand, Zur (2002a), an experienced practitioner, offers the following case to support his argument that some dual relationships can work:

Jack and I have played basketball for several years in our local recreational league. His wife, Janet, and I chaperone our children on field trips together and are on the same educational committee. When they called me seeking help to save their marriage, I delivered my sermon about dual relationships, objectivity, and ethical guidelines. In short, I told them I was not the man for the job. I had taught ethics, research, and clinical courses at the graduate and postgraduate level for over a decade, and my sermon was polished and substantiated with quotes, references and court cases. To my surprise Jack and Janet were outraged rather than being understanding: 'we have known you for a long time', they said, 'we know your values and how you treat your wife, your children and your friends. We know of several marriages you have helped put on the right path. We choose you *because* we know you and *because* you know us well.'

(Zur, 2002a: 44–5; original italics retained)

It was important to the clients that they knew Zur and already had a degree of trust in his capacity to be an appropriate therapist for them. Prior knowledge was a positive and crucial influence in selecting their therapist. Zur (2002a) also notes how when he moved to a small town in California, he had great difficulty coming to terms with the fact that people chose him as a therapist *because* they knew him. This was anathema to his counsellor training. Soon, however, he began to realize that to practise in a small-town setting necessitated overlapping therapy and non-therapy boundaries.

Zur and Lazarus (2002) helpfully highlight the fact that in some communities, it is not feasible or desirable to expect or aim for therapist anonymity. As they see it, to argue against client–therapist familiarity, suggests fear of the client discovering the practitioner's shortcomings or weaknesses. They associate dual relationship prohibition with therapist aims to minimize contamination of the client–practitioner transference relationship.

NON-SEXUAL DUAL RELATIONSHIPS, TRANSFERENCE AND COUNTERTRANSFERENCE

The concepts of transference and countertransference are widely recognized in psychoanalytical and psychodynamic approaches.

Arguably, in various guises transference (unconsciously motivated re-enactments and interactions in a present relationship through the medium of past relationship influences and events) and countertransference (the distortion of the therapist's perception and experience of the therapy relationship by their archaic psychological material) are present in some form in the majority of therapy approaches. Some have imbued the concepts with immense potency and significance. According to Kahn, these concepts 'lay[s] before the therapist a remarkable opportunity, not only for learning the secrets of the human mind, but for helping the patient as well' (Kahn, 1997: 35). While, arguably, Kahn's claim might seem grand, the idea that other relationships (past or present) as well as an individual's inner psychological material can influence their experiences and perceptions of a current relationship is certainly persuasive and in various guises is present in most therapy approaches. Significantly, this suggests that it is both necessary and appropriate to consider significant relationships and their potential impact on a dual relationship situation. The complex dimensions of the client–practitioner relationship with all its past, present and here-and-now material, and the multifaceted relationship, suggest a challenging situation that needs holding and managing.

Hedges (1997) points out that duality is an inherent aspect of all human relationships, thus the challenge is to find ways to work with this, rather than ignore it. Rather than shy away from relational duality, he appears to embrace it in his working concepts and practices and points out that the concept of duality forms the backbone of dynamically oriented therapies (Hedges, 1997). Essentially, the real or person-to-person relationship between client and therapist and the client's transference relationship (the re-enactment in a present relationship through the medium of past relationship influences) with the therapist constitute an unavoidable duality within the context of the therapy. Thus, from Hedges' analytically informed position it is only through the resolution of this duality that personal growth can occur for the client. Hedges claims, furthermore, that dual relationships *per se* are not the problem, rather it is therapists who are unable to deal with duality, or those who intentionally abuse, that generate problematic dual relationships. To this we might add those therapists who unintentionally are abusive in dealing with duality and dual relationships. In contrast to Hedges, Baer and Murdock (1995) suggest that the client or patient will be unable to resolve transference manifestations with a therapist who is also with them in some other capacity. They regard a dual relationship as anathema to successful resolution of the transferences. It would appear that while, on the one hand, some believe the matter can be reduced to a case of ethical management of the relationship situation (Hedges, 1997), paradoxically, others claim the situation can never be successfully mediated (Baer and Murdock, 1995).

Opposition to dual relationships is associated with psychoanalytical or psychodynamic orientations, but for Freud and his contemporaries, as well as some of his successors, it was common to have contact with patients outside the consulting room (Masson, 1985; Lazarus and Zur, 2002). Analyst Melanie Klein analysed her own children. Key figures from other approaches also engaged in similar behaviour. Yalom would sometimes visit clients in their home (Yalom, 1989) while Nina Coltart enjoyed social contact with her clients (Syme, 2003). The practitioners might well have believed that extending treatment boundaries into non-therapy contact was in the clients' interests. Recent evidence, however, suggests that clients in non-sexual relationships with their current or past therapist can experience feelings and responses to the situation that are similar to individuals who have been sexually abused by their therapist (Gabriel, 2001c).

Although the idea that the therapy relationship itself is dual or multifaceted is not widely featured in the counselling and psychotherapy literature, it is not a novel concept in therapy theories. Beginning with Freud (1962), theorists and clinicians have alluded to the multiple dimensions of the therapy relationship. As noted earlier, Greenson (1967) noted the co-existence of reality-based and transference-based dynamics in the therapy relationship. In turn, Clarkson (1995) incorporated Bordin's (1979, 1994) concept of the working alliance with her thinking and ideas from humanistic psychology, psychoanalysis and social constructionist thinking to form an integrative approach to therapy theory and practice that forms the basis for her UK training courses for counselling and psychotherapy practitioners.

According to Clarkson (1995), she has constructed a postmodern, contemporary approach that acknowledges the multiplicity of relationship types and functions that co-exist within the overall client–therapy relationship. In practice, she uses the concepts of transference and countertransference as conceptual tools to aid her thinking about the therapy relationship. Her multidimensional frame allows the practitioner to hold in their mind the different types of relationship that she believes operate in any client–practitioner relationship. These include the working alliance, the transference relationship, the person-to-person relationship, the developmentally needed/reparative relationship and the transpersonal relationship. As appropriate, the practitioner can call on these to inform their thinking and interventions. In relation to thinking about and dealing with dual relationships, then, her work might suggest the possibility of a flexible, multidimensional approach for dealing with these relationships.

On the other hand, Langs (1976, 1978, 1982, 1988, 2004) offers a counterpoint to any flexible or lax approaches to client–practitioner contracts and contacts. This differs from the more flexible and multidimensional approach that Clarkson (1994; 1995) advocates in relation to complex relating, such as dual and multiple role relationships. Langs argues for clear ground rules and treatment boundaries that delineate the patient–therapist relationship (Langs, 2004). A secured frame enables deep unconscious needs and motives to be held and explored through free association (saying whatever comes to mind), supplemented with guided associations (for example, working with dreams) (Langs, 2004). Distention, contamination or distortion of the secure frame negatively impinges on the therapeutic process and its effectiveness. While Langs suggests that minor challenges to the frame can be processed within the therapy relationship (Langs, 2004), a dual or multiple role relationship would severely rupture the work and relationship. Such a 'deviant' frame (Langs, 2004) would be anathema to helpful psychotherapy and counselling. Much of clients' and therapists' deep unconscious processes are unknown, contributing to a complex dual relationship situation that is not only deviant, but also dangerous territory. Langs's latest text (Langs, 2004) provides an accessible narrative on his theory of secure frames, deviant frames and ways in which deep unconscious processes might arise in helping work and relationships.

NON-SEXUAL DUAL RELATIONSHIPS IN THE CONTEXT OF A RESEARCH INQUIRY

An area where we are seeing reports of dual roles between client and therapist is counselling and psychotherapy research that overlaps current or past therapy work. Two significant contributors to the growing literature on this subject are Etherington (2000) and Wosket (1999). Both Etherington's and Wosket's work pioneers a proactive stance between the client–research contributor and the therapist–researcher roles. Both argue persuasively for a client-focused approach to researching therapy practice with current or past clients and exemplify research work undertaken by practitioners in order to advance their practice (McLeod, 1999a).

In Wosket's case, she researched the client and therapist experience of the process of therapy, using a procedure guided and prompted by sentence stems derived from narrative research approaches (Rennie and Toukmanian, 1992). An example of this might be seeking what the client found helpful or/and hindering about the therapy session. Following each therapy session, Wosket and the client independently completed their review, but the documents were not discussed during the life of the therapy relationship. According to Wosket, she sought to undertake research that took account of the vicissitudes of clinical practice yet remained meaningful and relevant (Wosket, 1999: 74). In her justification of researching the therapy process with a current client, she notes that a valid research contract between client and therapist:

> should not demand that the requirements of the study in any way compromise the therapeutic requirements of the counselling contract . . . It is only as we are able to forge approaches to research design and methodology that dovetail comfortably with the values and practices of the clinician that we can hope to heal the long term breach of the researcher–practitioner divide.
>
> (Wosket, 1999: 74)

In addition, she suggests that the research can work with the support of good supervision for both the academic and counselling content of the work. As she notes:

> I was fortunate in having a research supervisor who was research active. If this had not been the case, it would have been important for me to have access to another person who could supervise the research element of my work with this client and who could safely and fearlessly patrol with me the interface between counselling and research.
>
> (Wosket, 1999: 77)

Clearly, Wosket was both willing and able to use her supervisory relationship to help her explore the process and impact of the research on both the therapy and research dimensions of the client–therapist relationship. In particular, the supervisor provided helpful challenges to her decisions and actions. It would seem that the supervisor role was critical to the successful management of the situation and played a significant part in dealing with research choices and conflicts that threatened to impinge on the overlapping client–therapist relationship. On this occasion, the duality of therapy relationship and research roles appeared to work well.

Etherington's (2000) work reports on researching aspects of the therapy work of two past clients. Her narrative text incorporates prose, poetry and transcript extracts from discussions with her research collaborators/ex-clients and provides an insightful account of the experience of therapy–research duality and how it can be dealt with. Her text is from the perspective of both the client and the researcher and shows how the research process both enhanced the quality of her work as a practitioner and affirmed and encouraged the client–research collaborator. As she states in her discussion of collaborative working, '[L]ike any relationship, we need to dialogue and address the conflicts if the relationship is to be healthy' (Etherington, 2000: 187).

Although the exemplary work of these practitioner–researchers personifies effective qualitative inquiry with current or past therapy clients, their published representation of their investigations does not address in any depth the client's perception and experience of the client–participant dual role. We might inquire how an individual in the role of researcher–practitioner can be sure that the client *truly* consents to the research process. In view of the notion of 'demand characteristics' (McLeod, 2001: 178) that are thought to operate in some research contexts, this is a key question for qualitative inquiry involving dual roles.

Researcher–participant conflict might also arise when the researcher is also an experienced practitioner. During my research study, my own dual role, that of *researcher–practitioner*, became a cause for concern. The experience of forming a brief research alliance with one particular participant highlighted the importance of being clear at the outset about the boundaries of my role, as well as the limits of confidentiality in the researcher–participant alliance. We vaguely knew one another in a professional capacity, having met at training events. She heard about the project and was keen to participate. Following the interview, she expressed a fear that I might judge her as an incompetent practitioner and that this might influence how I perceived her in any future encounters. Since it was possible that we might meet at training events or through other professional activities, it was important to agree on how we might greet one another in a non-research context. This experience highlighted the importance of clear boundaries in the researcher–participant roles and informed my decision that beyond the pilot phase I would recruit participants that I did not know.

As a practising therapist researching a therapy-related topic, I approached the research investigation with a history of having worked with potent and conflicted material in the setting of a therapy session. However, within the context of the research interview, I experienced conflict between my therapist and researcher roles and background. Perhaps this is not surprising since, as Beauchamp and Childress (1994: 441) point out, 'the dual roles of research scientist and clinical practitioner pull in different directions and present both conflicting obligations and conflicting interests'.

Social psychologists see role conflict as a source of stress for those involved in roles that carry different expectations and obligations, especially when the obligations of one role are incongruent with those of another role. Arguably, however, unavoidable role conflict occurs for the therapist investigating counselling and psychotherapy, involving tension in the pull between the goals and focus of the researcher role and the obligations and responsibilities incumbent upon researcher when they are in a practitioner role. We do not leave our experiences and skills at the threshold of research interview setting. Relatively little exists about situations of researcher role conflict in counselling and psychotherapy research. Thomas chose to define her role as 'a counsellor first' (Thomas, 1994) when she undertook research work with her own clients and faced the challenge of reconciling her clinical practice with the demands of academic research. When researching experiences of adult male survivors of childhood sexual abuse, Etherington (1996) experienced the dilemma of competing role obligations in relation to what remains confidential to the research interview. More recently, Hart and Crawford-Wright (1999) argued that the literature does not address ethical concerns about overlap between research and therapy.

While on the one hand, I knew my research aims and focus were the priority in the context of the research interview, on the other hand, I felt morally obligated to be prepared to deal with any distress a contributor might experience as a result of participating in the interview. On the several occasions a contributor became distressed in the interview context, without seeking to transform the meeting into a therapy session, it was important to use helping skills to support the person to move on in the research meeting – and ensure that they were in a fit state to move away from it.

Arguably, we can construe therapeutic skills as helpful research resources to draw on as and when necessary. At a minimum, they possess the potential to aid interviewing. By this, I do not mean that the research interview becomes a counselling interview. Rather, I am suggesting that it is a meeting in which my counselling skills can be used in a context-appropriate way. Nonetheless, this is easier to strive for than execute. What helped me to stay focused in my interviews was to aim for a researcher stance of 'compassionate distance' (Beauchamp and Childress, 1994) and hold in mind the purpose of the meeting. Arguably, failing to acknowledge a participant's emotional distress constitutes a failure to uphold the moral principle of non-maleficence. Coyle argues a similar position:

> it verges on the unethical for a researcher to address sensitive issues with respondents, re-stimulate painful experiences, record them and then simply depart from the interview situation.
>
> (Coyle, 1998: 57)

How, then, could I as researcher respond to a participant's distress in a way that respected the individual, yet did not lose sight of the purpose of the interview? In other words, how could I hold the research alliance in a productive yet compassionate way? As I saw it, within the interview context, I needed to remain focused on the research question as a means of holding the research focus. The approach outlined in the list below shows some of the ways in which I sought to support myself and the research participants through the interview process.

Ways to minimise and contain researcher–practitioner role conflict

Provide clear information for contributors
- Give details of research
- Seek full and informed consent

- Offer information on the possible consequences of participation; offer the contributor the opportunity to withdraw their contribution at any time
- Outline the researcher role at interview

Form an effective research alliance
- Undertake clear initial contracting and boundary setting
- Be compassionate in the researcher role – adopt a stance of 'compassionate distance'; strive to achieve a balance between an impassioned and impassive stance
- Attend to maintaining a good enough balance in the research alliance between bond/task/goal elements of the alliance (as per Bordin (1979; 1994) model)
- Consider any evidence/suggestion of parallel processes between research processes and research topic
- Communicate type/limits of post-interview contact

Have a clear policy on confidentiality
- What is disclosed to a researcher within the context of the research interview, for instance, remains in confidence; disclosures are not treated as subject to the responsibilities and obligations that might be incumbent upon the researcher in any other therapy-related role they fulfil, such as counsellor or supervisor
- Be clear about limits of confidentiality and when consultative support is required

Cultivate self-reflexivity
- Regularly review researcher role/research process and practitioner–researcher dichotomy – through self-reflection, supervisory meetings, peer/collegial meetings, etc.
- Use ethics codes, moral principles, problem-solving models, etc. as consultative sources to inform decision-making and actions
  Source: Gabriel, 1999

Seeing my role as, on the one hand, a recorder of the contributor's narrative, while on the other hand, a facilitator who might draw on counselling skills where appropriate, helped me to hold the focus and purpose of the research meeting. While that was my explicit aim, there were times when holding the tension between researcher role and aim and practitioner past and experience was difficult. I knew that I did not construe the interview context as a cathartic arena in which the individual explored their dual relationship experience, but rather, saw it as a storytelling space, in which I, as researcher, was present to facilitate and witness the individual's telling of their experiences and perceptions. Clearly, as I argued above, parallels exist between an in-depth research interview and a therapy session, but there are critical differences. In particular, the explicit nature and intent of the research context differs from that of a counselling session. For example, in the research interview, I was creating a space in which contributors gifted their story and although my subsequent analysis and interpretation of the collective of contributors' stories would embody individual stories, ultimately I held authorship of the stories. Conversely, in a therapy interview context, ownership of the client's story remains with the client.

In my researcher role, then, the process, content and form of the interaction between myself and the contributor is monitored as I attempt to hold my researcher–therapist knowledge and experience and aim for a collaborative combination, rather than perceiving the situation as a clash of conflicting roles. However, the ease with which I narrate this process does not, perhaps cannot, adequately capture the challenges and complexity of the lived experience.

When researching our own client group, how can we *really know* that the client *truly consents,* rather than defers to the wishes and requests of their therapist–researcher? It is helpful to bear in mind that research suggests that clients are willing to be critical of their therapists in research interviews with a researcher, yet reluctant to disclose their concerns with their therapist because of the need to be seen to support the therapist (McLeod, 2001). For example, questionnaires issued to clients at the end of therapy might contribute to responses dominated by a wish not to undermine the reputation of the therapist who has done his or her best to help the client (McLeod, 2001). Clearly, this generates difficult but important questions about the client's experience, impression and willingness to disclose their true perceptions. Clients can defer for a number of reasons including fear of criticising the therapist, concern about the therapist's approach, or a wish to meet the therapist's perceived expectations (Rennie, 1994a). Moreover, the notion that clients feel subjected to 'demand characteristics'

(McLeod, 2001) suggests that in a dual relationship a client might well say one thing, yet mean another – potentially dangerous territory for both client and therapist.

Chapter 5

Roles and boundaries in dual and multiple role relationships

The boundary in counselling can be perceived as a limit line, with inherent fluidity and permeability, as well as safety and security. It is a limit line that requires the thoughtful actions of the *boundary rider*, the counsellor, to monitor and repair where necessary in order, as far as is possible, to ensure security and safety.

(Gabriel and Davies, 2000: 37)

Crossing the boundaries of therapy relationships into other roles and contexts forms the basis of a major argument against dual relationships – that to do so engenders boundary and role conflict. Psychodynamic theory places emphasis on the significance of relationship boundaries and their holding and containing purpose (Holmes, 2000; Langs, 2004). We see it as the practitioner's role and responsibility to provide a 'safe space' for the client by introducing and maintaining secure boundaries of place and time (Holmes, 2000).

Counselling and psychotherapy, irrespective of theoretical orientation, are 'relational activities' (Eatock, 2000; Mearns and Thorne, 2000), thus are interactive and dynamic. The complex interactions and role and boundary overlaps that are likely to be involved in dual or multiple role relating suggest that the concept of 'role' is more than merely a title or description. It is also a 'function'. The notion of a relationship 'role' refers to the behaviour expected of, and associated with, a person who holds a particular position (McLeod, 1998). A practitioner's role responsibilities and expectations when she is in the role of 'therapist' might differ markedly from social norms associated with a friendship relationship that she also has with her client. Undoubtedly, theoretical orientation will play its part, along with the personal characteristics of the therapist and client, in shaping what constitute the 'norms' for a given relationship.

In his work on the therapy relationship, Tudor (1999) points out how the concept of *relationship* can be confused with that of *role*. Since these are significant but ambiguous concepts in relation to dual relationships, it is helpful to define them here. The *Oxford Reference Dictionary* (1986) defines 'role' as 'actor's part; what a person or thing is appointed to do'. This definition implies expectations and obligations that can be associated with a particular task, purpose or function. Bringing these ideas into the realms of helping relationships, *role* can be seen as:

> a relational activity *and* position that carries with it certain expectations and obligations (that is, role tasks) on the part of the therapist as well as the need for certain relational capacities and abilities in order to be able to fulfil these.

The term *relational* refers to the conditions and interactions of the relationship, while *relationship*, according to the *Oxford Reference Dictionary* (1986) is a 'state of being related; condition or character due to being related'; and 'kinship'. *Kinship* is about being in relation with another (*Oxford Reference Dictionary*, 1986), so a *therapy relationship* is one where the client and therapist enter into contracted and narrative relations with one another. It is important to distinguish between the concept of *therapy relationship* and *therapeutic relationship*. I define a *therapy relationship* then, as:

> a contracted relationship between a person in the role of client and a person in the role of therapist for the express purpose of entering into narrative relations aimed at resolving the client's 'problem' or helping them develop their goals.

On the other hand, I see a *therapeutic relationship* as:

> one of a number of types of relationship that are experienced as healing or beneficial by one or both individuals involved. For example, these could be friendship, colleague, mentoring or social types of relationship.

Because of the therapist's role obligations that form an explicit or tacit part of a contracted therapy relationship, the *therapy relationship* becomes, arguably, the *primary* relationship. Dual or multiple roles that overlap therapy and non-therapy contexts will be *secondary roles* (Pope and Vasquez, 1998).

The status and classification of roles and relationships that occur *prior* to the therapy relationship need to be decided. Therefore, it might be appropriate to decide that the *primary* relationship is the *first* relationship formed between the two individuals. So, for example, giving primacy to the first relationship, which happens to be a friendship, will impact on the quality, progress and processes of a subsequent therapy relationship between the individuals. By regarding therapy as the primary relationship, then questions of whether and how to suspend the friendship over the course of the therapy will be significant when deciding whether or not a dual relationship is appropriate

ROLE IDENTITY

The idea of 'non-therapy' and 'extra-therapy' roles and relating is a useful way to think about extensions to the therapy work and relationship and distinguish between contracted therapy and non-therapy roles or matters. I regard non-therapy contact as client and therapist interactions that are completely separate from the contracted therapy work and relationship. On the other hand, I see extra-therapy contact as an extension of the therapeutic work and as part of the contracted therapy relationship. Broadly speaking, therapists of a humanistic orientation are more tolerant of extra-therapy and non-therapy contact, while analytical approaches are less so, although within the analytical field, exceptions exist, with Langs (2004), for example, suggesting a combined therapy and supervisory relationship for the experienced psychotherapist. Humanistic approaches tend to perceive human beings, almost always, as fundamentally trustworthy, while traditional psychoanalytical thinking sees humans as a constellation of unpredictable and irrational intra-psychic drives that need to be contained and controlled.

We assume that professionals who fulfil significant helping roles will act in role-appropriate ways. Individuals who enter into a therapy relationship hold the ascribed roles of 'client' and 'therapist'. As previously noted, a major tenet of the arguments against therapists' taking on a dual relationship rests on the capacity for role anxiety and conflict to arise (Kitchener, 1988) because of the overlap with non-therapy roles. Some opponents use social psychology's role theory to support their argument that because of the potential for role conflict, dual roles are inadvisable (Kitchener, 1988). The kind of relational complexity that exists in complex dual or multiple role relationships would run counter to approaches that regard psychological duality or multiplicity as pathological (Rappoport, Baumgardner and Boone, 1999; Rowan and Cooper, 1999). Some psychological states are diagnosed as split, multiple or borderline personalities, yet postmodern views in psychology increasingly acknowledge and give primacy to the multifaceted and relative nature of the self (Rappoport *et al.*, 1999).

Conflict arises when competing roles are perceived as incompatible by one of the 'role players'. According to Secord and Backman (1974), the more similar or compatible roles are, the more easily they assimilate and the less likely it is that role conflict will arise. 'Pay-offs' can complicate an individual's capacity to change or challenge the dual or multiple role relationship. According to Wrench (1969), individuals both imagine and/or receive rewards for conforming to role expectations and punishments for violating them. He classifies the conflicting expectations that stem from holding two different roles and their associated obligations as *inter-role* conflict and claims it can be avoided by judicious choice of role positions, although fails to expand on ways of making such choices. Far more challenging, he claims, is *intra-role* conflict. Here, the role-holder and other individuals differ in their expectations of the role. This fuels role anxiety and creates interpersonal problems. Secord and Backman (1974), argue that taking on a new role requires the role-holder to learn a new conception of self in *that* role. In order to be accepted in a new role, a person 'has to learn the norms and rules which usually go with the role' (Strongman, 1979: 232). Conflict is most likely to arise where an individual is involved in roles that carry different expectations and obligations (Kitchener, 1988). McLeod argues that one of the guiding principles of counselling is to:

> avoid allowing role conflicts to occur in relation to a client . . .
> it is generally considered bad practice for a counsellor or
> therapist to be a friend, colleague or relative of a client, since

the expectations and behaviours elicited through these other relationships will get in the way of the counselling relationship.
(McLeod, 1998: 299)

Role conflict is thought to be one of the reasons why it is difficult to establish counselling agencies in rural settings, since it is likely that 'everyone knows everyone else and the kind of anonymity required for role "purity" can be impossible to guarantee' (McLeod, 1998: 299). McLeod queries the negative connotations attached to role conflict and suggests that, in some circumstances, it might actually be a valuable experience for a client to learn about and work out the implications of different role expectations he or she held in relation to the counsellor (McLeod, 1998). In addition, it is also crucial that a therapist can work out his or her role obligations and expectations of the relationship and client, as well as have some understanding of the impact of additional non-therapy roles. At one point early on in my practitioner experience, I worked with clients from minority communities. I soon realized the challenge of overlapping connections when at a party. I was settling into the party when the flow of conversation was halted by the arrival of another guest – one of my clients – in a drunken state. To my horror she made straight for me, flung her arms around me and proclaimed her great pleasure at seeing me! After this event I decided to avoid the local Turkish baths, fearing unexpected encounters in the steam room!

On the other hand, individuals might need to develop their capacity to withstand role ambiguity (Welfel, 1998). Looking beyond the traditional dyadic therapy situation to other types of helping relationships we can identify some interesting and alternative ways of conceiving 'role' and the experience of being in roles in psychodrama. Moreno, an early twentieth-century psychiatrist, developed and used psychodrama as a medium for psychological integration and growth (Moreno, 1947). He conceived the dual nature of 'self', which he saw as represented through inner, psychological 'roles' and an outer social self that interacted through various roles with others and the external world. Focusing on a more socially constructed notion of 'self in the world', Goffman (1959: 16) defines 'role' as 'the enactment of rights and duties attached to a given status'. This notion is mirrored in Sarbin's (1954: 225) definition of role as 'a patterned sequence of learned actions or deeds performed by a person in an interaction situation' and his argument that a 'fully functional' or psychologically healthy person can effectively and appropriately enter into a range of roles. Subsequently, Sarbin and Allen (1968) identified three significant dimensions of role enactment: number of roles; role sequence; and role involvement. The greater the capacity of the individual to play multiple roles, the more able the person is to deal with a wide range of social circumstances. The idea that capacity to sustain multiplicity and complexity correlates with relational competence seems plausible.

According to Landy (1993), roles constitute mediating functions for humans and satisfy a range of physical, social, cultural and psychological needs. Psychodrama, dramatherapy, counselling and psychotherapy explore the human dilemma of individuals struggling with crucial issues of their existence (Landy, 1996). Landy usefully presents a way of understanding role behaviour that places paradox, ambivalence and change at its centre. Problems are thought to arise when roles conflict and this can trigger anxiety, fear and shame. Essentially, his approach supports an individual to become role fluent. One of Landy's central assumptions, shared by existential orientations, is that although human beings seek balance and integration, they live in a world of conflicting psychological and social forces that can lead to emotional imbalance (Landy, 1993). Clearly, if we are unable to mediate between roles, problems will develop.

Although counselling and psychotherapy probably have a long way to go in developing explanatory and pragmatic theories on dual relationships, oganizational and management theory might be further ahead in identifying pragmatic ways to deal with role issues and conflicts. Handy (1993) argues that when individuals do not give clear information about their role they risk confusing or antagonizing others. This fosters assumptions and misplaced responses and can result in feelings of insecurity and lack of confidence. Therefore, if a role is not distinct through some form of *role sign*, the other person involved may not react in the appropriate way and a cycle of assumptions can begin. From this perspective, it is not too difficult to imagine how negative, inaccurate perceptions might affect the interaction. Handy (1993) also usefully separates out *role conflict* (conflicting roles) from *role incompatibility* (conflicting expectations), but claims *role stress* always results. With such potential for confusion and misplaced assumptions, it is not too difficult to imagine how a dual relationship situation could become conflicted and stressful.

ROLE AND RELATIONAL BOUNDARIES

As noted earlier, it is widely accepted that the therapist is responsible for ensuring that the boundaries of the therapy relationship are appropriately maintained (Barnet, 1996; Bond, 2000; Simon, 1992; Smith and Fitzpatrick, 1995; Webb, 1997). Perhaps unsurprisingly, the complexities of actually dealing with relationship boundaries in dual relationships can provoke anxiety in therapists (Gabriel, 1996). Unfortunately, these therapist anxieties often remain hidden and the impact on the client is relatively unknown. Notably, few publications mention the client's understanding or experience of therapy *per se*, although a few clients have documented their reactions to the therapy relationship or therapists with 'loose' or 'firm' relationship boundaries (see, for example, Elliott and Williams, 2003; Heyward, 1993; Sands, 2000).

In relation to distinguishing between roles, Webb (1997) believes that in order to reduce actual or potential boundary mismanagement, therapist training must place the topic of dual relationships on the curriculum. She suggests that Western European cultures and traditions have much to learn from other cultures about the handling of more than one relationship between the same individuals. Citing examples from Samoan culture, she usefully notes how different personal titles ascribed to different relationship roles provide a ritual way of helping people set aside other roles while a particular one is being enacted.

Using ritual to delineate roles seems a creative way of holding complex relationships. However we manage relationship roles, we need to take account of the context in which the relationship exists. For example, in case-managed services (common in a UK, NHS context) Morgan usefully describes 'boundary slippage': 'there is a constant temptation to slip into ambiguity as a result of drifting from the professional relationship into that of friendship' (Morgan, 1996: 75). In this instance, slipping into ambiguity equates with role confusion and blurred boundaries. Conversely, he also suggests the possibility of a different interpretation:

> it can be an essential part of the therapeutic nature of the interventions to be constantly discussing these boundaries and limits with the client. If we identify interpersonal relationships as being a frequent area of difficulty for people, then the very

nature of discussing and highlighting boundaries and limits should act as an intervention targeted to a specific need.

(Morgan, 1996: 75)

The idea of boundary discussions between client and therapist also allows for the idea of a relational mutuality that involves explicit sharing of power and responsibility for relationship decisions and actions. Morgan (1996) makes the point that there need to be clear relationship boundaries in order that we can:

1   identify what constitutes the helping relationship and distinguishes it from other types of relationship;
2   determine needs for confidentiality and expectation of appropriate behaviours;
3   set realistic expectations on outcomes;
4   acknowledge that a hierarchy often exists in the relationship, despite any attempts to mitigate this situation; and
5   determine the need for onward referral or discharge.

In addition, we need to consider how and when does the former client cease to be regarded as 'client'? Is it a case of 'once a client, always a client'? Any reading or representation of dual relationships needs to engage with the question of whether, when and how the therapist ceases to regard the client as his or her 'client'. The identity and role of *therapist* and *client* are ascribed certain attributes, expectations and obligations by the therapist, the client and the counselling and psychotherapy profession. When and how do the qualities and duties associated with the roles of 'therapist' and 'client' cease to operate? For instance, should a client formally cease to be regarded as 'client' when the therapy relationship ends? In relation to possible contact with former clients, BACP has previously noted that:

> Counsellors remain accountable for relationships with former clients and must exercise caution over entering into friendships, business relationships, sexual relationships, training, supervising and other relationships. Any changes in relationship must be discussed in counselling supervision. The decision about any change(s) in relationship with former clients should take into account whether the issues and power dynamics present during the counselling relationship have been resolved.
>
> (BAC, 1998: B.5.3)

A parallel view is expressed by Pipes (1997), who argues that therapists should responsibly and carefully consider their obligations to former clients. What seems to be a central concept is our ability to instigate reasoned thinking and decisions about when and how a client ceases to be seen as the 'client' and identify an appropriate way to mark this. Backlar (1996: 505) suggests that therapists need to learn 'the three Rs: roles, relationships and rules' and argues that 'judgement is a peculiar talent that can be practised only, and cannot be taught' (Backlar, 1996: 509).

BOUNDARY RIDERS

Despite the fact that boundaries are discussed in counselling and psychotherapy and the wider mental health literature, actually defining 'boundary' is no easy matter. Therapists tend to intuitively understand the concept, yet have problems explaining what it is (Gutheil and Gabbard, 1993). This uncertainty might underlie opposition to dual relationships on the premise that the relationship boundaries are difficult to manage. Conversely, therapists might not create opportunities to think through their own definition and understanding of 'boundary'. Since 'boundary' defines the limits of the helping relationship, we need to understand and interpret the concept within the relational context.

Gabriel and Davies (2000: 37) interpret 'boundary' as a moveable limit and argue that it is the responsibility of the therapist, the 'boundary rider', to monitor and manage the limits of the therapy relationship. The 'boundary edges' of the relationship comprise the complex relational obligations and interactions that occur in the session-to-session and moment-to-moment actions and decisions (Gabriel, 1996). Hence, the counsellor in the role of boundary rider (Gabriel and Davies, 2000) faces a complex quest in their endeavours to secure and monitor the relational boundaries. They are the sentinels of the process.

Dealing with overlapping relationship boundaries presents challenges for those who live and work in minority community contexts (Gabriel, 1996). As Gabriel and Davies (2000: 37) note, 'the reality of living and practising within one's community can resemble that of a small town, where interconnections and knowledge of the inhabitants are shared'. Gay therapists who choose to live and work in the same locale face difficult decisions on managing relational boundaries. In the box below, Gabriel and Davies (2000: 47–50) offer a challenging scenario on encountering clients in social settings. It is a complex and difficult scenario. The practitioner's cultural and moral values are significant features. Obviously, where minority culture and prevailing beliefs and ethics codes appear to clash, the therapist may face a major ethical and moral dilemma. As was apparent in the case below, managing dual relationship boundaries can be anxiety-inducing and stressful for therapists who live and work in sexual minority communities (Gabriel, 1996; Gabriel and Davies, 2000). Yet, to avoid overlaps within what is often a complex network of interconnecting relationship contacts is anathema to many sexual minority therapists. They are more likely to argue for culturally sensitive practice that embraces diversity (Gabriel and Davies, 2000; Neal and Davies, 2000; Sue and Sue, 2003) and accounts for the intentionality of the practitioner in pursuing a dual relationship.

A social encounter

A gay therapist engages in 'backroom' or group sex gatherings. During one gathering, he finds himself face-to-face with a client. After some composure time, the therapist begins to think clearly. He recognizes he might have breached his code of ethics and regrets not having explored the possibility of overlapping boundaries during the contracting phase of the therapy relationship and resolves that in future he will be clear with clients when exploring the likelihood of social contact. He considers his options and decides to privately acknowledge the situation with the client, seek agreement to discuss the situation at their next therapy session and leave the gathering. He reflects on the situation and recognizes that the client might feel the relationship has been irrevocably damaged by this encounter and might prefer to continue his therapy with another therapist.

Gabriel and Davies (2000) helpfully suggest that this situation can be redeemed and argue that mutually processing the situation with the client, as well as drawing on supervision, can support appropriate responses. They also refer to Gabriel's (1998) suggestions for managing unplanned overlapping contact.

Working with dilemmas in dual relationships and overlapping connections

Stage 1: Impact and containment

Immediate actions:
- Contain shock and impact of situation;
- Invoke stress/crisis management techniques;
- Contain any immediate 'fallout'/acting-out impulses;
- Invoke an 'internal supervisor';
- Make contact with the client, acknowledging the situation;
- Seek agreement to discuss situation at the next therapy session;
- Model healthy, appropriate behaviour.

Stage 2: Containment and processing

Intermediate actions:
- Acknowledge situation at the next therapy session;
- Discuss with client issues of confidentiality, boundaries, overlapping connections, and possible rehearsal of agreed actions should another situation arise;
- Address client's reactions/responses to the situation;
- Address transference issues;
- Provide ongoing containment;
- Redeem the therapeutic alliance;
- Discuss countertransference reactions in supervision and personal therapy.

Stage 3: Ongoing processing

Longer term:
- Explore transference and address countertransference in personal therapy and supervision;
- Work with issues triggered by or linked to dual or multiple roles and relationships.

(*Source*: Gabriel, 1998)

Difficulty with accepting and living with paradox and complexity might account for some of our ambiguity around dual and multiple role relating. In a professional or social culture that counsels prohibition, a practitioner may struggle to understand a non-sexual dual or multiple role relationship they are participating in, yet fear discussing the situation in supervision. They might be unwilling to disclose this shift for fear of some form of 'retribution'. Alternatively, if a practitioner's relationship with a current client develops a sexual dimension, they may be unwilling to disclose this in supervision, fearful of the consequences of disclosing.

Discussions so far suggest a need for practitioners to develop their capacity for *reflexive practice*. According to Rennie (1998), reflexive thought and action is an essential skill for therapists – one that promotes the ability to critically yet compassionately take reasoned decisions and actions in their work. This suggests an attitude to client–therapist non-therapy contact that is less about avoidance and more about finding the right attitude and approach (Wosket, 1999). Undoubtedly, this demands an awareness and understanding of the relational boundaries (McGrath, 1994). A central human quest involves finding ways to deal with the ambivalence and paradox of being in relationship. Developing a capacity to sustain oneself across a range of roles would play a significant part in achieving this. In a dual relationship, then, client and therapist would inhabit their various roles and reflexively respond to the inevitable conflicts and challenges that arose.

Chapter 6

Dual relationships and relational ethics

> Helping without hurting . . . [O]ur ethics acknowledge the great responsibilities inherent in the promise and process of our profession. They reflect the fact that if we do not fulfill these responsibilities with the greatest care, people may be hurt.
>
> (Pope and Vasquez, 1998: 1)

All helping professions expressly or implicitly promote client protection. The medium through which the counselling and psychotherapy profession most evidently and explicitly promotes its duty of care is practice ethics. Professional registers such as the UKRC (United Kingdom Register of Counsellors), ethics codes and frameworks from bodies such as UKCP (United Kingdom Council for Psychotherapy) or BACP (British Association for Counselling and Psychotherapy) and the values and stance that they espouse, constitute the current self-regulated approach to ethically sound practice in counselling and psychotherapy. The codes embody principled statements of required or advised actions and attitudes in helping relationships.

The ethical resources produced by professional bodies are not static entities but are subject to revision according to professional and social circumstances. With the prospect of statutory regulation for the UK counselling and psychotherapy profession not far off, it is reasonable to assume that the ethical and moral integrity of the practitioner will come under far greater scrutiny than at present. It is also conceivable that regulation might mean the government and professional bodies will insist on a uniform understanding of dual relationships. At best, this can promote ethical mindedness and actions on the part of the professional in a dual relationship with a current, former or possible future client, as well as promote a degree of confidence in the quality of the professional's 'goods and services' on the part of the therapy consumer. Unfortunately, at worst, scrutiny might push 'predatory professionals' (Pearson and Piazza, 1997), struck off the register, say, for an abusive dual relationship, to the very fringes of therapeutic work, where the unscrupulous individual is currently free to set up in private practice.

Aside from professional codes, there are few pragmatic guides bringing ethics into counselling and psychotherapy practice. However, recent publications suggest the situation is improving, with more resource texts becoming available (see for example, Clarkson, 2000; Gabriel and Casemore, 2003; Jones, Shilloto-Clarke, Syme et al., 2000; Palmer Barnes and Murdin, 2001). Nevertheless, we cannot rely on texts alone. Therapy training, supervision and continuing professional development (CPD) have a significant role to play in providing an environment in which a practitioner can develop skills and competencies for ethical and effective therapy. Otherwise, how might practitioners and clients negotiate the tricky ethical and moral terrain of dual relationships? BACP's (2002) framework offers helpful pointers, in that it promotes ways of thinking and behaving thought to be critical for effective and ethical practice. Briefly, the frame refers to moral principles as well as virtues, values and personal characteristics for effective and ethical therapy work and relationships. However, for those struggling to deal with a challenging dual relationship, the framework does not offer explicit means to achieve these ends; consequently, it is down to the practitioner to formulate an inter-pretive ethical framework. Unless their training equips them to respond to ethical and moral issues or they are in supportive and appropriately challenging supervision, then the practitioner and their clients are at risk. While supervision might not necessarily pick up ethical breaches, where there is a relationship of trust, it is more likely that the practitioner will disclose issues.

MORAL PRINCIPLES UNDERPINNING HELPING WORK AND RELATIONSHIPS

In the day-to-day lived experience of a dual or multiple role relationship, a practitioner and their dual relationship partner must decide what is acceptable, appropriate or harmful and find his or her own way through the minutiae and lived reality of the relationship. With little explicit guidance, practitioners can turn to moral principles to inform their thinking and actions. Therapy relationships, overtly or tacitly, come under the influence of moral principles that underpin client–practitioner relationships in the majority of the helping professions (Beauchamp and Childress, 1994). The key principles that inform codes and guidelines for practice are:

- *autonomy* – encouraging and allowing a client's capacity for free and independent thinking;
- *beneficence* – action for the good of, and in the best interests of, the client;
- *non-maleficence* – refrain from harming the client;
- *justice* – doing what is fair; and
- *fidelity* – being faithful to the fiduciary relationship between client and therapist that is based upon trust.

In the client–therapist relationship, the principle of autonomy and the related notion of informed consent are important features of the relationship, although we do assume a degree of client competence to make reasoned choices (Betan, 1997). Where a client cannot or does not do this, then the therapist's capacity for manifesting the remaining principles is crucial. Proctor (2002) offers a perturbing insight into a client's experience of not being able to summon up the courage to make her own choices:

> I believe that I finally managed to leave therapy only because, after four and a half years, my therapist did not seem to object to the idea or to continue to interpret my desire to leave as my running away from something. It felt that carrying out my decision to leave was based on whether she agreed with the 'rationality' of my decision. In retrospect, this concerns me very much when I realize how my autonomy, consent and responsibility for my own decisions were compromised to such an extent.
>
> (Proctor, 2002: 122)

It took Gillian Proctor several years of therapy before she was able to make the decision to leave. From her experience, we can envisage the difficulties that some clients involved in a dual or multiple role relationships might have. In counselling and psychotherapy, we espouse client autonomy, confidentiality and well-defined relational boundaries, yet Proctor's story provides a clear example of a practitioner not affording or promoting client autonomy.

Our emphasis on autonomy and individual agency has been significantly influenced by counselling's roots in humanistic philosophy and psychology and the work of formative figures such as Carl Rogers. Alone, however, principles are inadequate and need translation through some form of pragmatic framework. As Thompson asserts:

> by adopting a principles-based approach, codes direct practitioners to judge the rightness and wrongness of acts independently of the particularity of the situation and the moral agency of the people involved. In doing this, the situation is disembedded (stripped of context) and the 'subject' is disembodied (depersonalized).
>
> (Thompson, 2002: 522)

Some form of decision-making framework that accommodates the situated experience (that is, the dual relationship) will help. Without it, we might rely purely on intuitive responses to the situation or event, which may be inadequate or inaccurate (Kitchener, 1984; McLeod, 1998; Meara, Schmidt, and Day, 1996). Undoubtedly, intuition plays a valid and valuable part in our relational decisions and actions, yet needs some form of integration with other psychological and decision-making approaches. We can develop our 'ethical mindfulness' (Bond, 2000) through drawing on decision-making models to inform our thinking and practice, as well as working with hypothetical cases to build our capacity to appropriately respond in challenging situations.

A number of ethical decision-making models now exist in the counselling and therapy literature (see, for example, Bond, 2000; Gabriel, 1996; Gabriel and Davies, 2000; Gabriel and Casemore, 2003; Robson, Cook, Hunt et al., 2000). A useful US model focuses on practice ethics in educational contexts (Anderson and Davies, 2000) and Herlihy and Corey (1992) offer a model that involves a cost–benefit analysis of the situation. In addition, there is an increasing drift towards developing culturally and socially relevant models for working with ethical issues (Meara et al., 1996; Sherwin, 2001). All of the models build on existing knowledge and theories of ethics and incorporate the moral principles outlined above. They communicate a multidimensional approach to decision-making and reduce problem-resolution and decision-making processes to a number of critical stages. Although they are helpful resources, as 'flat' linear models they need to be 'brought alive' in some way for the practitioner. For example, case studies or role enactments within training or supervised postgraduate practicum contexts might provide useful ways for practitioners to practise and develop their skills.

Despite being widely accepted in the helping professions, practice principles are not without their critics. They have been condemned when embodied in a rule-based ethic that attends to the abstract at the expense of the situated or local experience (Gilligan, 1982; Koehn, 1998). However, in relation to dual relationships, given the weight of evidence of client damage by these relationships, a prohibitive stance based on the principle 'do no harm' should not be surprising. Nonetheless, we need to develop ethical approaches that leave space for respecting alternative individual, collective and cultural positions on moral and theoretical perspectives (Sherwin, 2001).

VICES AND VIRTUES: THE HUMAN THERAPIST

In addition to a principled approach to practice ethics, the personal qualities, virtues and characteristics of the individuals involved will influence the quality and outcome of the relational situation or event. Human beings are not perfected machines but fallible creatures. That said, as Pope and Vasquez (1998: 63) suggest, therapists 'must know their own emotional strengths and weaknesses, their needs and resources, their abilities and limits for doing clinical work' and develop what they term 'emotional competence' (Pope and Vasquez, 1998: 63).

US research suggests that the therapist's unique personal history is likely to impact on their therapy work and relationships (Pope and Feldman-Summers, 1992). How a person's history influences their capacity to be effective in helping relationships is an under-researched area (Wosket, 1999). Nevertheless, previous research suggests that a significant number of practitioners might have experienced some form of abuse. Pope and Feldman-Summers

(1992) found that nearly one third of male therapists and two-thirds of female therapists had experienced some form of abuse in their lifetime. Of these, 21.05 per cent of the women and 5.84 per cent of the men reported childhood or adolescent sexual abuse by a relative. The concept of the 'wounded healer' (present in some analytical schools, particularly Jungian) depicts the human therapist's emotional and psychological 'wounds' and acknowledges their potential impact on the therapeutic relationship and processes. However, what seems central to a successful encounter with one's wounded healer is the capacity to know and acknowledge the wounds and be aware of how they influence the client and helping relationship. It is here that supervision and peer relationships, self-monitoring and personal development can be important influences on how we attend to our 'wounds'. While some therapy approaches require their practitioners to be in personal therapy, there is no conclusive evidence that it is effective as a means of attending to our 'wounds'. However, as one dimension of maintaining our fitness to practise, many would argue its benefits.

It seems that to admit to being less than competent is tantamount to acknowledging failure as a therapist. This is especially so in the prevailing professional culture that prioritizes and prizes 'competence' (Vaspe, 2000). The impact of this is evident in the silence that surrounds erotic transference and the difficulty around disclosing information perceived as unorthodox or possibly unethical. Concerns about erotic transference can present a dilemma for those therapists who are subject to sexually themed advances from clients, or who find themselves sexually attracted to their clients (Stirzaker, 2000). However, in the context of contemporary counselling and psychotherapy practice, it is gradually becoming less acceptable to deny aspects of professional practice that border on the unorthodox and more acceptable to disclose personal psychological wounds (Page, 1999).

In addition, although the notion of unorthodox practice has received little attention in the literature, it is likely to be a feature of many therapists' work to varying degrees (Wosket, 1999). Indeed, some years ago, McCartney (1966) noted how two significant figures in the US therapy field publicly declared and advocated certain 'accepted' professional behaviours, while they privately behaved in different and unorthodox ways. Evidently, the old adage 'don't do as I do, do as I say' seems to apply in a number of publicized cases. However, where does that leave the therapist struggling to work in an authentic, respectful way with clients with whom they have entered into a dual relationship?

NOTIONS OF 'RIGHT' AND 'WRONG' THERAPIST CHARACTERISTICS AND ACTIONS: THE GOOD, THE BAD AND THE UGLY

We assume that therapists will strive towards 'right', principled actions rather than 'wrong' practices. Yet, whether intentional or unintentional, people will offend or make mistakes. The identification of therapists who are deemed 'duality offenders' and a system of 'offender rehabilitation' exists in the therapy field in some US states (Celenza and Hilsenroth, 1997). Moreover, there is now the notion of 'offender profiles' (Schoener, 1999). Drawing on existing US research, Schoener's (1999) outline of factors present in sexual abuse of clients by psychotherapists and other helping professionals implies that offending behaviour exists on a scale from minor to major misdemeanours. Those who offend are thought to fall into a wide range of categories, ranging from a healthy person with some sort of situational breakdown in judgement, to a lifelong predator (Schoener, 1999). Factors thought to be present in cases of therapist abuse of clients include:

- inadequately trained, or inadequately trained for a particular role or setting;
- poorly defined job description with inadequate orientation, and inadequate supervision;
- lack of good supervision or failure to use it;
- lack of understanding of power differential, transference or countertransference;
- low self-esteem with excessive need for client approval;
- naïve and lacking in good social judgement;
- some form of organic impairment caused by medication;
- impaired judgement secondary to alcoholism or drug addiction;
- emotionally needy and dependent;
- suffering from some form of psychological disorder – for example psychopathology; borderline personality; impulse control disorders;

- the wounded healer – the therapist is situationally needy or impaired due to some life event.

While not all of these factors are likely to be present in a single case, some of them are easily recognized life events or features that could confront any of us who are practitioners, at any point over the course of our working life. A key consideration seems to be how we deal with the event or situation. Potentially abusive non-sexual relationships might arise in a variety of situations. For example, problems could arise when course tutors are also therapists. Syme (2003) considers some of the difficulties that can occur, including transference and countertransference problems, conflicts around where session material should be taken, separating out the different contexts and introducing potentially destructive dynamics into course assessment. In addition, it is possible that cult figures and 'groupie' dynamics could be set up where a practitioner acts as therapist, trainer, supervisor, friend, business associate, and so on. This has occurred in the US and UK therapy field.

The US therapy profession is more accustomed to dealing with high-profile cases of abusive dual relationships and practitioners appear to have adopted a defensive attitude, perhaps in order to pre-empt potential litigation claims. In the US there is a more litigious culture than here in the UK at present. The US certainly has a history of prominent litigation cases against offending therapists and an established therapist rehabilitation programme for those who do offend. Perhaps the apparent UK reluctance to more publicly identify and rehabilitate dual relationship 'offenders' might rest partly on the taboo, undisclosed nature of this type of relationship, as well as a cultural reluctance to 'blow the whistle' on offenders. However, unless dual relationship cases (good *or* bad) are openly debated, how can we identify exemplary or problematic approaches for dealing with dual relationships? Although this question assumes that both 'good' and 'bad' dual relationships exist, typically the professional literature depicts only those deemed 'bad'. Nevertheless, the recent edited volume from Arnold Lazarus and Ofer Zur (Lazarus and Zur, 2002) aims to redress this imbalance. They offer a number of anecdotal accounts of the positive benefits of being in a dual relationship. For example, Zur (2002a, 2002b) will frequently associate with clients (past, present and potential clients) outside the therapy context in social, friendship or business settings.

According to POPAN (1999), the characteristics of a bad therapist include the misuse of their authority, a failure to maintain appropriate relationship boundaries and the use of therapy relationships to meet their own psychological needs. Thus when these characteristics prevail, exploitative actions are more likely to occur. Although it may be easy to assume that a newly qualified (or inexperienced) therapist is more likely to find themselves in this type of situation, the contrary can also be true. In fact, POPAN found from its experiences of advocating for complainants that even very well trained therapists can run into problems when working with more challenging clients (POPAN, 1999). However, practitioners' problems tend to remain hidden or unspoken until forcibly exposed through complaint or litigation actions.

Although there may be potential benefits to being more open about our vulnerabilities, inadequacies or fears in dual relationships, prevailing arguments constrain individuals from disclosing their own and others' dual relationship experiences. Perhaps it is difficult to openly acknowledge our personal and professional limits. Openness probably requires a facilitative context – one in which it is permissible to acknowledge personal limitations, failings or vulnerabilities. Obviously, one of the major benefits of open discourse on dual relationships would be to challenge, deconstruct and reformulate myths and misperceptions that therapists must be seen to be perfectly competent in their work at all times. Nevertheless, strong opposition threatens the willingness to disclose details of one's dual relationships or relational issues. The immense power of this deterrent is exemplified in Kagle and Giebelhausen's argument that:

> Practitioners found to have engaged in any dual relationships should have their licenses or certifications revoked and their memberships in professional associations terminated.
>
> (Kagle and Giebelhausen, 1994: 218)

For some individuals, this statement is likely to prevent their speaking out about dual relationship questions or concerns. The line between disclosure and exploration that is acceptable and an individual's responsibility to report on ethical transgressions is far from clear. It is difficult to find out what takes practitioners into dual relationships and how they manage being in these relationships. Obviously, there are well-publicized cases that suggest the therapists involved fall into Pearson and Piazza's 'predatory professional' (Pearson and Piazza, 1997) category but not all therapists or dual relationships will fall into abusive categories.

However, Pope (1988a, 1988b) cynically asserts that *any* justification of dual relationships is reducible to a defence against unethical behaviour and thus raises doubts about the integrity of the therapist. Our logic of justification, then, appears to be crucial. Not everyone takes Pope's position (see, for example, Syme, 2003; Lazarus and Zur, 2002) yet it is realistic to ask those who choose to be in a dual relationship whether they are fully aware of their motives and intent. For example, in seemingly unavoidable dual relationship situations, do individuals explore the options to ensure that the 'unavoidable' status is apt? If so, and they choose to continue, will they consider the various issues and strategies for dealing with the relationship?

Questions about the virtuous (or otherwise) nature of an individual and the role of attitudes and emotions in moral and ethical decision-making and actions are examples of what Beauchamp and Childress identify as 'character ethics'. As they (1994: 69) point out:

> When the feelings, concerns, and attitudes of others are the morally relevant matters, rules and principles are not as likely as human warmth and sensitivity to lead us to notice what should be done.
>
> (Beauchamp and Childress, 1994: 69)

From this perspective then, the therapist's compassion, humanity and sensitivity in the relationship, as well as their capacity to be aware of the needs of both the situation and the client, are central to effectively dealing with the situation. This way of approaching the relationship embodies an ethic of care, similar to that espoused in feminist positions on ethics. Thus, the client's responses to the dual relationship and its associated situations would be respected and regarded as important relational feedback that might help inform subsequent responses or interventions in the therapy relationship, as well as any overlapping roles. It would seem then, that the therapist's character will make a significant contribution to the quality and progress of the dual relationship. Consequently, it might be appropriate to suggest that the therapist's relational integrity and ability to deal with the relationship is paramount.

RELATIONAL INTEGRITY

By *relational integrity* I mean the practitioner's capacity, intent and obligations in the therapy relationship. This includes providing relational conditions that are conducive to and facilitative of the client's resolution of presenting issues. We might imagine that virtues such as trustworthiness would be present in the relationship. This does not mean pursuing the notion of becoming some form of mythical 'perfect therapist', but suggests striving to critically and compassionately work through relational decisions, actions and interventions. These expectations of professional helping relationships are found to varying degrees across the broader context of the medical professions where there is a long-standing tradition, dating back at least as far as the formation of the Hippocratic Oath, that the integrity and trustworthiness of the practitioner is assured by the profession and can be assumed by the consumer/client.

Of course, this line of reasoning assumes the practitioner's capacity to provide appropriate and necessary relational conditions for therapeutic change. The faith of the client in the therapist and the faithfulness of the therapist over the course of the relationship are central tenets of helping relationships across most helping professions. However, as prominent public cases of professional misconduct or abuse testify, at times this implicit trust and duty of care fails. A legitimate concern of dual relationship opponents relates to the challenges of holding and maintaining an appropriate ethical and moral distance between client and therapist.

Where a relationship carries the risk of harming the participants, there are then major ethical and moral issues, responsibilities and consequences to consider. This line of thinking brings into focus the notion that a therapist needs to develop sufficient confidence and competence in order that they can ethically problem-solve and sustain themselves through conflicted, chaotic or paradoxical situations. However, as Dickenson (1991) argues, there is an element of moral luck in any ethical decision or action and we might need to remember that moral certitude does not exist. A recent survey of UKCP registered psychotherapists indicated that they had difficulty when confronted with complex relational and ethical situations (Lindsay and Clarkson, 1999). Not only were there anxieties around dealing with the complexities of social relationships with clients, there was also ambiguity about how to respond when a colleague was involved in what they perceived to be an unethical relationship with a client.

The notion of 'whistle-blowing' (Purtilo, 1999), of disclosing what we believe to be a colleague's exploitative behaviour, is a relatively new idea in the counselling and psychotherapy profession, but actively encouraged in the medical profession as a means of discouraging unethical practice. However, 'whistle-blowing' might be present within the counselling and psychotherapy profession in other guises. For example, supervision serves a monitoring and reporting role as well as a supportive function, although the supervisor's beliefs, decisions and interventions in response to alleged or actual unethical practices will be influenced by their theoretical preferences. In addition, the complaint and grievance procedures of professional bodies constitute a form of 'policing'. That said, it is *self*-regulation that currently applies, with its implicit assumption that practitioners will strive not to abuse their personal or professional power in their relationships with clients. It would seem then, that the integrity of the practitioner is crucial.

Arguably, relational integrity involves an awareness of the personal and interpersonal dynamics in the relationship. Holmes and Lindley (1991) believe that non-analytical therapists need to be aware of transference and countertransference and their ethical implications, because of the critical awareness they can bring to a practitioner's understanding of the therapy relationship. Essentially, they claim that by invoking these concepts, some of the ethical dilemmas of therapy can be resolved. Accordingly:

> because therapists are inevitably important figures in their patients' lives, and because emotional arousal is a central issue in most therapies, 'everyday' transference is likely to be an ingredient in them, whether recognized or not. When difficulties arise in therapy it is often because transference and countertransference are not being acknowledged. If this is so, it is important for non-analytic therapists to ensure they are aware of transference and countertransference.
>
> (Holmes and Lindley, 1991: 117)

Transference can be positive or negative. Where the therapy relationship is construed as a friendship, the emphasis is likely to be on positive transferences, thus the opportunity to explore the negative transference is removed. From this position, then, in a dual relationship involving overlapping relationships premised on a positive transference, such as some friendships, collegial or business relationships, the negative dynamics in the relationship might be manifested in unconscious ways that adversely influence the relational dynamics. Since the therapist's first duty is to provide a secure frame or 'containment' for the client, this predicament is anathema to most analytical approaches (Holmes and Lindley, 1991).

We can witness some of our ethical and moral concerns about complex relational situations in the concerns of counsellors and psychotherapists who work in multi-tasked jobs. For example, complex and diverse professional roles are increasingly evident in managed care contexts, bringing therapist and client into extended contact across a range of tasks, purposes and contexts. Practitioners have issues associated with the integrity of their client work, often based on how they believe the situation compromises client autonomy and confidentiality, as well as concerns about dealing with relational power and role boundaries (Gabriel, 2001b). Multi-task or multi-role practice demands that the practitioner be a 'boundary rider' (Gabriel, 1996; Gabriel and Davies, 2000). Given that the demands of multi-task work appear to generate similar relational issues and dilemmas to those encountered in dual and multiple role relationships, the notion of the boundary rider can apply in each domain.

Chapter 7

Client and practitioner dual and multiple role relationships

In this chapter, I offer the reader a brief outline of the findings from the research into client and practitioner experiences of dual and multiple role relationships. Tables with summaries of clients' and therapists' dual relationship experiences are included, while more detailed narratives on client and practitioner experiences are included in Chapters 8 and 9.

KEY FEATURES OF CLIENT AND PRACTITIONER DUAL AND MULTIPLE ROLE RELATIONSHIPS

A summary of key findings about the dual or multiple role relationship:

- the relationship can have beneficial as well as detrimental outcomes;
- a non-sexual dual relationship can be as damaging as the reported affects of sexually abusive relationships between clients and their past or current therapists; equally, some non-sexual dual relationships can be beneficial;
- finding a way of being in dual or multiple role relationships can be traumatic and damaging for some individuals; equally, there are others who appear able to mediate between dual or multiple roles;
- not only can dual relationships harm clients, they can also harm therapists;
- conflicts can arise from the context in which the relationships occur;

- the successful dual relationships appeared to be predicated on a positive emotional bond; where the bond is evident in the life of the therapy relationship, this can influence the decision to pursue further roles and relationships;
- concurrent dual relationships appeared to be more difficult to deal with than sequential relationships;
- there are complex issues of role identity and relational responsibility and obligations in dual relationships.

Key features of the client experience:

- the client's emotional reactions to the relationship could be of epic proportions and a roller-coaster nature;
- some clients withhold their thoughts and reactions to the relational situation and remain silent about their experiences;
- complex relational dynamics can be involved; for example, the client might feel special in the relationship as a result of being favoured by the therapist and be reluctant to threaten their 'special' status and the 'pay-offs' it brings;
- some clients experience conflict and ambiguity about breaking silence and speaking out about experiences of non-sexual relationships;
- clients encountered problems associated with concerns or conflicts arising from role transitions, boundaries, confidentiality;
- clients who found dual relationships beneficial or positive seemed more able to sustain themselves in the relationship;
- clients in successful or beneficial relationships appeared to be more psychologically robust;
- although a client might assent to the dual or multiple role relationship, they might not fully understand its implications or the relational complications and costs;
- the findings show that it is possible for some clients to thrive in dual relationship conditions; the conditions for 'thriving' or 'failing' appear to vary according to the individuals involved, the contexts in which they relate and the type of roles in which they are engaged.

Key features of the therapist experience:

- a therapist might be unable or reluctant to take their dual relationship issues to supervision; this might be for various

reasons, including doubts about the capacity of the supervisor or some fear, guilt or shame about being in the relationship;
- some therapists experience conflict and ambivalence about breaking silence and speaking out about experiences of non-sexual relationships;
- therapists in successful or beneficial relationships appeared able to deal with the conflicts and challenges of the relationship and the contexts in which it occurred;
- where the therapist uses some form of client assessment, the quality and outcome of the relationship is thought about in advance and thus the therapist is more aware of the possibilities or pitfalls;
- therapists encountered problems associated with concerns or conflicts arising from role transitions, boundaries, confidentiality.

The client participants

The clients ranged in age from 30 to 60 years, with eighteen women and one man. I did not set out to locate equal numbers of men and women client contributors, but it seems notable that only one male client came forward. Cases where clients felt harmed by the dual relationship did not appear to fit any gender pattern. For example, both male and female therapists were involved in cases where the client felt harmed. While the sample size is too small to make general claims, nonetheless it is possible to speculate. The majority of the client contributors were women. Given that there was only one male in the client contributor group, it might suggest that more women than men are harmed in a dual relationship. Equally, it might also suggest that in non-sexual dual relationships, more women therapists are involved. In addition, it could suggest that women are more willing than men are to come forward and discuss their dual relationship experiences. Additionally, counselling and psychotherapy is largely a white, middle-class profession, largely populated by women practitioners, who are, perhaps, more inured to disclosing their emotional response and experiences. However, as stated earlier, these can only be speculative comments.

Speculation about the gender splits has to be cautious, but it is interesting to note that most statistics on sexually abusive dual relationships show that where abuse occurs, it is usually the case that female clients are exploited in therapy relationships with a male therapist. Fifteen of the clients were in a dual relationship with a female therapist, three were in a relationship with a male therapist and the one male client was in a relationship with a female therapist. While research seems to indicate that most female clients are abused (sexually) by male therapists, in this investigation, in the three cases where the female client was in a relationship with a male therapist, two of them experienced it as beneficial. The third client experienced her male therapist as psychologically abusive. In addition, all were recounting stories about non-sexual dual relationships. Although the gender of the dual relationship partners might be significant to the experience and outcome of the relationship, it is difficult to comment authoritatively on the extent of its impact.

A significant feature about the client-contributors is the fact that at the time of their contribution, they were in practice as therapists. However, at the time of their dual relationship experiences, some were either untrained or trainees. While it could be claimed that a trainee therapist or a trained therapist reflecting on their dual relationship might be sensitized to psychological concepts and clinical practices, nonetheless I was seeking contributors who were able to articulate their dual relationship experiences. I do not regret recruiting client participants from a wider therapist population, but realize that this choice affects the research outcomes. For instance, it raises questions about whether and how the stories of the client-contributors that are included here might differ from those clients who have no prior understanding of counselling and psychotherapy, or who may not be sensitized to psychological talk and concepts. Clearly, they were people who were willing to talk openly and honestly about their subjective experience of being in a dual relationship. Of course, it is a wholly different scenario if we seek the views of vulnerable adults and there certainly were cases of individuals who clearly were threatened and harmed by their dual relationship experience. These are key considerations for any similar future investigation.

As you will see from the client experiences in Table 7.1, the relationships occurred across a wide range of contexts. Those in multiple role relationships obviously encountered the widest range of roles. For example, the first client shown in Table 7.1, who had a very damaging experience, first encountered her dual relationship partner in a trainee–trainer relationship. It then developed into social contact, then business contact, then into a therapy

Table 7.1   Client (*n*=19) experiences and perceptions of dual relationships: the overall relationship quality and the range and number of roles

Overall quality of relationship	Range of roles	Number of roles	Relationship scope: the primary (first) relationship and subsequent secondary roles
Largely negative	Multiple	7	Friendship, then staff member/line-manager roles; trainee–trainer relationship, therapy relationship, supervision relationship, other work roles and group therapy roles
Largely negative	Multiple	5	One-to-one therapy relationship, then overlapping couple therapy, then subsequent trainee role with overlapping supervisee role, colleague roles and business roles
Largely negative	Multiple	4	Friendship relationship, then overlapping work roles, trainee role and supervisee role
Largely negative	Multiple	4	Therapy relationship, then overlapping couple therapy, then trainee role and overlapping supervisee role
Largely negative	Multiple	4	Trainee–trainer relationship, then overlapping therapy relationship and social and educational contact
Largely negative	Dual	2	Therapy relationship, then overlapping work roles
Largely negative	Dual	2	Therapy relationship, then overlapping trainee role
Largely negative	Dual	2	Therapy relationship and overlapping fellow student roles
Largely negative	Dual	2	Complementary therapy relationship, then talking therapy relationship and overlapping complementary therapy relationship
Mix of positive and negative experiences	Multiple	4	Therapy relationship, then subsequent trainee role, then colleague role and overlapping supervisee role
Mix of both positive and negative	Multiple	4	Participant in a personal development group facilitated by therapist, then one-to-one therapy relationship with overlapping trainee role and some social contact
Mix of both positive and negative	Multiple	4	Therapy relationship, with overlapping pastoral, social and community contact and a developing friendship relationship

(*continued*)

Table 7.1   (Continued)

Overall quality of relationship	Range of roles	Number of roles	Relationship scope: the primary (first) relationship and subsequent secondary roles
Mix of both positive and negative	Multiple	3	Therapy relationship, then overlapping colleague roles and student roles
Mix of both positive and negative	Multiple	3	Therapy relationship, then overlapping social and family contact
Largely positive	Multiple	5	Complementary therapy relationship, then overlapping therapy relationship and trainee role, and social and community contact
Largely positive	Multiple	3	Therapy relationship, then overlapping trainee role and social contact
Largely positive	Dual	2	Therapy relationship with overlapping non-therapy contact in professional context
Largely positive	Dual	2	Trainee–trainer relationship, then subsequent therapy relationship
Largely positive	Dual	2	Therapy relationship, then subsequent friendship relationship

relationship, then supervisee–supervisor roles and finally, work/ collegial roles.

The therapist participants

The therapists' ages ranged from 30s to 70s, with thirteen women and five men. It is interesting to note that more male therapists came forward than male clients. As noted earlier, my research was exploratory and not designed to evaluate any gender split in contributors, but it might be significant information to bear in mind for future investigations of dual relationships. Eleven of the therapists were in a dual relationship with a female. Of the male therapists, two were in a dual relationship with a woman, but the quality of the relationships varied, with no seeming pattern in the male/female mix in the relationships.

The therapists' counselling and psychotherapy qualifications ranged from a counselling certificate through to psychoanalytical training. Their theoretical orientations ranged from humanistic, through existential, CBT (cognitive-behavioural therapy), NLP (neurolinguistic programming) and integrative to an orthodox analytical approach. Contributors located themselves across a number of professional identities, including: counsellor; psychotherapist; psychologist; doctor; trainer; mentor; coach; welfare officer; and supervisor. Several contributors held more than one of these role identities.

The context in which the therapists' relationships occurred varied widely and included secure units ($n=2$), NHS centres or primary care teams ($n=3$), organizations ($n=9$), private practice ($n=15$), voluntary sector ($n=2$) and training institutes ($n=3$). Of those who worked in private practice, several also worked in other therapy contexts. Of the 18 therapist contributors, 9 were involved in dual relationships in some form of organizational context. Four of these worked in multi-role jobs. For example, a welfare officer might first encounter the individual in an advisory or advocacy capacity then, over the course of their contact with the client, the work develops into one-to-one therapy. Alternatively, contact might first occur through one-to-one therapy work, which then leads into other types of roles or contact in the organization. For instance, it was common to meet clients in recreational or social areas of the organization, such as canteens. Collegial roles accounted for 22 per cent of the therapists' primary relationships. The second most prominent type of initial contact was a therapy relationship, which accounted for 17 per cent of the relationships. Many of the relationship roles overlapped chronologically, with new roles developing while others were already in place. Four therapists had multi-role, complex and convoluted relationships while the remaining fourteen were dual role relationships. The therapists subscribed to BACP, BPS, UKCP and ITA codes of ethics and conduct and their number of years in practice as a therapy practitioner were in the range 2–35.

Nine therapists found the relationship a largely negative experience, four a largely positive experience and five a 'mixed' experience (see Table 7.2). Those who had a largely negative, or bad, experience tended to encounter role conflicts, boundary management problems and work-related stress. Those who had a largely good experience had relationships that were characterized by what seemed to be a higher degree of awareness (this applied to both therapists and clients), assertive relating, appropriate knowledge and skills (in particular, problem-solving and decision-making) and evidence of seeking and facilitating mutuality, equality and equity in the relationship.

Table 7.2   Therapist (*n*=18) experiences and perceptions of dual
relationships: the overall quality of the relationship and the range and
number of roles

Overall quality of relationship	Range of roles	Number of roles	Relationship scope: the primary (first) relationship contact and the subsequent secondary roles
Largely negative	Multiple	3	Facilitator relationship with a group member, then overlapping advocacy and then social/friendship contact develops
Largely negative	Dual	2	Teacher–student relationship then overlapping one-to-one therapy relationship
Largely negative	Dual	2	Colleague roles then overlapping therapy relationship formed
Largely negative	Dual	2	Custodial relationship initially, then overlapping therapy relationship
Largely negative	Dual	2	Colleague roles, then subsequent therapy relationship
Largely negative	Dual	2	Initial welfare role with client, then overlapping therapy relationship formed
Largely negative	Dual	2	Initial welfare contact with overlapping therapy relationship
Largely negative	Dual	2	Therapy relationship, then subsequent brief social contact
Largely negative	Dual	2	Peers in a developmental group context, then overlapping one-to-one therapy relationship formed; one-to-one ends and group contact continues
Mix of both positive and negative experiences	Multiple	3	Trainer–trainee relationship initially, then overlapping supervisory role, following end of these, subsequent therapy relationship formed
Mix of both positive and negative	Dual	2	Members of pastoral community with overlapping therapy relationship
Mix of both positive and negative	Dual	2	Trainer–trainee relationship, then overlapping therapy relationship
Mix of both positive and negative	Dual	2	Therapy relationship, with overlapping social and community contact
Mix of both positive and negative	Dual	2	Therapy relationship, with overlapping friendship and social contact

(continued)

Table 7.2   (Continued)

Overall quality of relationship	Range of roles	Number of roles	Relationship scope: the primary (first) relationship contact and the subsequent secondary roles
Largely positive	Multiple	3	Colleague relationship, then co-counselling and mentoring relationship and overlapping friendship
Largely positive	Dual	2	Colleague relationship, then overlapping therapy relationship
Largely positive	Dual	2	Colleague relationship, then overlapping therapy relationship
Largely positive	Dual	2	Friendship relationship then overlapping therapy relationship

Unlike the client-contributors, none of the therapists contributed by correspondence. Many of them seemed keen to contribute, in person, to what they saw as an important and under-represented topic. As noted in an earlier chapter, none of the therapists who contributed spoke of a sexually oriented dual relationship. On two occasions, individuals who were in what appeared to be non-abusive sexual relationships with former clients made contact with me, but neither were willing to be part of the investigation. While I can understand the therapists' and clients' choice, I also regret that no one who had been in a sexual dual relationship came forward.

An anonymous survey document might be more likely to generate a response, as it is a more remote form of participation and, unless survey documents are marked in some way, the individual is not traceable. For those who do not wish to disclose their identity this could be a preferable research method. In this investigation, however, individuals had to clearly identify themselves; an aspect of contributing that is likely to have prevented those who intentionally entered into sexual relationships from coming forward to contribute.

Although I asked the therapist contributors about their professional qualifications, I did not explicitly seek information about their training experience (in relation to whether or not the topic of dual relationships was included in their training curriculum). Several, however, did volunteer that the subject was not part of their training. The role and content of training in relation to dual relationship ethics and related matters might be an important point to include in a future inquiry.

The range, quality and nature of the dual relationships

The primary and secondary roles involved in the clients' and therapists' dual relationships covered a diverse range and quality. Before expanding on these, however, I want to define the terms 'primary' and 'secondary'. Here, the idea of the first, or primary, relationship denotes the initial contact between the dual relationship 'partners' (that is, the individuals who at some stage in the life of relationship take the roles of 'client' and 'therapist'). Thus, secondary roles constitute any other type of contact.

Thirteen of the clients' primary relationships were therapy relationships, while the therapists' occurred in a range of settings including therapy, work/business, training and welfare contexts. Clearly, it is possible to construe the concept of 'primary' in different ways and this was evident when a contributor placed greater value on a particular role or relationship, irrespective of the chronological order of the roles. For example, an initial friendship for one participant was the prime relationship, while for another person it was the initial therapy relationship.

Notably, twelve of the clients were in multiple role relationships. This might be significant, in that the more roles involved, the less able the client is to differentiate between the roles. Interestingly, however, five of the multiple role relationships were of a mixed type, that is, the client felt that there were both positive and negative aspects to the relationship. Only one of the largely positive relationships was of a multiple role type. In light of this, it is possible that the multifaceted relationship brings more conflict and challenge in terms of dealing with the various roles.

Beginnings, progressions and endings

How the dual relationship began varied markedly between the client and therapist contributor groups. The majority of the client relationships began as a therapy relationship. Of the nineteen clients, twelve began their relationship in this way. Of the remaining seven, one began as a friendship, three with the client as a trainee, two with the client in a complementary therapy relationship with the future therapist and finally, one where the client participated in a personal growth group with the future therapist.

An optimistic position and outlook characterized the beginning of the client relationships, but for those who felt that they had a bad experience, this perspective changed as the relationship became chaotic or conflicted in some way. Those with mixed experiences recounted more of an ebb and flow in the relationship, echoing how many human relationships progress. Few of their relationships were of a dual role nature, with many multiple role relationships ($n=12$) involving a number of diverse roles, including, for example, trainee, supervisee, employee, friend, business colleague and, of course, client. The greatest number of roles that the relationship progressed into was six. This is notable, since the majority of literature fails to clearly identify or account for multiplicity in the client–therapist relationship.

Many client dual relationships commenced as a client–practitioner relationship, yet paradoxically, therapists' dual relationships commenced in a variety of ways. Three began as a therapy relationship, four with the therapist and future client as colleagues and the remainder were friendship, advocacy or welfare work, or social or shared community contact. Some of the explicit motives for therapists having begun the dual relationship included the need to find placements for their therapy training. On these occasions, individuals in the workplace provided the 'placement'. Several of the therapists communicated the significance of the relational bond between themselves and the client that subsequently influenced a decision about whether or not to begin a dual relationship with that particular person. This notion of bonds and a sense of there being a 'kindred spirit' between client and therapist seemed to be a significant feature in these cases. In other cases, changes in workplace roles and obligations led to complex and conflicted dual relationships, including for example, cases where the therapist was also relating to the client in advocacy, mediation or advice-giving roles. In some organizational contexts, such as managed care or primary care settings, this type of multi-role job or overlapping roles appeared to be commonplace.

Relationship endings were less clear or evident than their beginnings. Many of the dual relationships were ongoing at the time of the research interview. Of those that were finished, the majority had an acrimonious or ambivalent ending. The apparent emotional impact on *most* clients and *some* therapists of their dual relationship experience was substantial, irrespective of whether or not the relationship was perceived to be good or bad. Significantly, dual relationships caused extensive emotional and psychological harm in several client cases and a few of the therapist cases. The narratives of clients who had a bad relationship experience showed how debilitating the impact could be. Moreover, and contrary to dominant perceptions and beliefs about dual relationships, these relationships can be harmful for therapists. Again, this was evident from the stories of those therapist contributors who reported an overall negative experience. The overall quality of the relationships ranged from good (or largely positive) to bad (or largely negative), with variations (a mix of positive and negative) in between. The relationships appeared to fall into a beneficial or harmful pattern, with nearly twice as many of both the clients and the therapists recounting a harmful or negative experience. However, it would be inappropriate to draw any conclusions or speculations from this pattern. The conceptual labels of 'harmful', 'damaging' or 'beneficial' suggest a parallel with the evidence from the literature and research discussed earlier; especially with regard to the US survey research and the in-depth UK work undertaken by Russell (1993). Both sources claimed that sexual dual relationships were damaging, with the US research indicating that non-sexual relationships were also harmful. In addition to this, there was literary and anecdotal evidence, suggesting that not all dual relationships were harmful or negative and that some might be beneficial. This appears to have been borne out by the findings, with five of the clients and four of the therapists reporting an overall positive or beneficial experience.

The fact that some of the clients had damaging experiences lends support to arguments against dual relationships based on the premise that they harm the client. Nevertheless, the findings also challenge these arguments, since the 'mixed' and 'good' experiences were clearly uncharacteristic of the usual depiction of dual relationships in the counselling and psychotherapy literature. Also contrary to dominant images and discourses of dual relationships, there were clients who believed that they had actually benefited in some way from the relationships. In addition, several of these individuals felt harmed to varying degrees by the relationship, yet were fearful about challenging the therapist about the relationship.

Ambivalence about the term 'dual relationship'

Uncertainty about dual relationship terms and interpretations was common among the client and therapist participants. In particular, the concept of 'dual relationship' was a frequent source of misinterpretation or confusion and there were a number of different definitions and constructions of the term ranging from any kind of overlap between therapy and non-therapy (from brief unplanned encounters to multi-tasked roles) to a close friendship relationship between a client and a therapist. Since no commonly held definition of dual relationship exists it is perhaps hardly surprising that this was reflected in the contributors' assumptions about, or interpretations of, the term. Equally, it probably highlights unfamiliarity with terms and suggests that dual relationships are inadequately discussed, either during therapist training at undergraduate or postgraduate level, or in the professional literature. While it is not possible to give a definitive taxonomy of dual relationships here, it nevertheless is clear from the client and therapist groups that potentially confusing, possibly unhelpful constructions or interpretations exist. For the purposes of this work, a definition of dual relationship was constructed in Chapter 2 and is repeated here for the reader's benefit:

> a one-to-one contracted therapy relationship between an individual in the role of 'client' and one in the role of 'therapist' overlaps into a non-therapy context or role. The overlapping contact could occur whilst there is a current therapy relationship, or before the therapy relationship is formed, or beyond its cessation. The non-therapy contact could be friendship, social, sexual, collegial, financial or business oriented.

CONCLUDING COMMENTS

None of the clients or therapists reported a sexual dual relationship. It is possible that those who were in a sexual relationship were unable to contribute, were unaware of the research, or were unwilling to disclose details of an 'abusive' relationship. Notwithstanding this, the findings show how, in non-sexual dual relationships, the client can feel abused and experience trauma in a similar way to those who have felt harmed by a sexual dual relationship. Several communicated their impression of the taboo nature of the relationship and their pleasure or discomfort about its 'secret' nature, while at the same time feeling guilt about the possibility of harming the therapist if they disclosed anything about the relationship – hence the section of the book title that claims to be 'Speaking the Unspeakable'.

Chapter 8

Client experiences of being in non-sexual dual and multiple role relationships

complex, multiple and powerful feelings – overawed, ideal-
izing, protected, special, favoured, affirmed, supported, safe,
encouraged, excited, hopeful . . . furiously angry, deceived,
cheated, used, emotionally, financially and psychologically
abused, shocked at the therapist's manipulativeness, rebellious,
manipulative, imprisoned, trapped, very frightened, helpless,
incompetent, depressed, despairing, deep shame that I couldn't
extricate myself, feeling that I needed the therapist.

(A client on her dual relationship experience)

A PASSIONATE PROCESS

The above words characterize one client's roller-coaster experience
of being in a dual relationship and set the scene for a potent story
of relational conflict and stress. Extreme, roller-coaster shifts
between love and hate, passion and pain, intimacy and abandon-
ment were common. However, not all relationships ended in
despair or damage and several clients saw their experience as
positive or beneficial. Irrespective of their overall impression of the
relationship, clients' experiences crossed a broad spectrum of
emotions ranging from positive to negative. Those who felt most
damaged by the process spoke of feeling worthless, paralysed,
despairing, afraid, ashamed, abused, or desperate, and some were
completely debilitated by the experience. Some shut down emotionally to defend against feeling their reactions in the relationship,
while others commented on being 'flooded' with powerful emotional reactions that hindered their capacity to respond to the
situation. Such responses could happen irrespective of the client's

own knowledge and experience of therapy and psychological processes. This client's experience was typical:

> although cognitively I knew that the action was wrong, I felt overwhelmed with longing and conviction that this and only this person could understand and help me.

An experienced therapist and trainer herself at the time of the dual relationship, nevertheless the relational events threw her into a distressed and anxious state. Despite her practitioner knowledge and experience, it was difficult to cope in the face of an emotionally challenging situation in which she felt confused and vulnerable. Angst about 'ways of being' in role was common, particularly in cases where the client had a damaging or hurtful experience. In the absence of knowing how to be in a role, it seemed commonplace to make assumptions about their obligations or what their dual relationship partner expected of them.

Stress and anxiety increased when the client's therapist did not appear to support them in the new relationship territory. For many clients the roller-coaster effect of powerful and extreme feelings led to them 'splitting off' their emotional and vulnerable self and shutting down that part of themselves in the therapy relationship and any associated overlapping dual or multiple roles. In several cases, confusion about thoughts and feelings led to a form of psychological paralysis involving a sense of immobilization and inability to respond. In other client cases, there was an intentional withholding of thoughts and feelings, for fear of losing the relationship, or making the situation worse. Several clients were in a dual relationship with a past or current therapist who failed to support them to find ways of dealing with their relational angst and conflict. In others, it seemed that the therapist might have provided secure conditions and in some respects they thrived in the dual relationship. However, separating out from the relationship partner and ending or losing relationship roles they had shared over many years was difficult, even when desired.

Several could not share their feelings with the therapist for fear of being rejected or ejected from the relationship or, in some cases, fear of not being believed – all of which could compound confused thinking, shame, guilt or self-blame at feeling or being unable to manage themselves in the situation. Consequently, they suffered in silence.

On a more positive note, five of the clients found the experience positive overall and a further five found it a mixed experience, involving beneficial and pleasurable aspects. In the two client stories shown below, Rachel's experiences characterize some of the difficulties, while Eve's story reflects a more positive perspective and experience of being in a dual relationship. Later in the chapter, we will look at themes that arose from the nineteen client participants' narratives.

Rachel

Although a fully trained therapist herself, the experience of becoming a colleague of her therapist was a damaging one for Rachel. She had been in therapy for around a year when her therapist informed her that she was to become her colleague, stating 'is that ok?'. Despite Rachel's 'yes, . . . that's fine, I don't mind' response, in retrospect, she felt completely unprepared for the actual experience of working with her therapist. The therapist's theoretical orientation was humanistic and the client wondered whether this played a part, since she seemed casual about the situation and appeared to assume that Rachel was ok about it.

Rachel noted how 'I couldn't be honest, I couldn't think there was going to be a problem with it at the time . . . when you're caught cold on the phone by somebody it's more difficult to get your thoughts together and recognize that it's going to take more deep thinking'. Once into their collegial roles, what Rachel found especially hurtful was the fact that her therapist did not check how she felt about their changed relationship situation. In particular, she found the times in the staff canteen excruciating and did not know how to place herself when she encountered her therapist-colleague in this informal social setting. Seeing Hannah as a colleague in the social setting, mixing with other staff was difficult:

> I feel a bit uncertain about what is their relationship with each other, would she maybe say something about me, and on a knowing level I know she wouldn't, but the child inside says, maybe she'll talk about me to her friend.

None of the other staff knew that their new colleague also happened to be Rachel's therapist. Rachel had made confidential disclosures to the therapist within the therapy context, as well as to colleagues in the canteen setting and found it difficult to know how, what and where to make further disclosures. The situation immobilized her. Like a rabbit frozen in car headlights, she did not know which way to turn. She had no sense of how to resolve the situation or move on from it and felt unable to share her uncertainty with the therapist. She felt betrayed and abused by her and thought that 'she could have said "how do you feel about me being there, how does it affect you?" and we could have started taking the lid off'. Her feelings were compounded when the therapist indicated she was likely to remain in the department. At no time had the therapist invited Rachel to share her feelings, issues, experiences or concerns about the situation. Nor, at that point, could Rachel volunteer her fears and concerns. From the context and content of their therapy work, Rachel thought that Hannah should have been more mindful of her predicament. She was aware of Rachel's emotional and psychological concerns and it was hard to reconcile this feature with Hannah's present behaviour. Rachel felt that the therapist failed to address her needs as the client in the dual relationship and was instead satisfying her personal desires. The unanticipated dual role was extremely challenging, affecting both her job and the therapy relationship. Effectively, she withdrew emotionally during therapy sessions, feeling the need to protect herself, and found it increasingly difficult to trust the therapist. She felt unsafe and had lost faith in the relationship, yet at the same time she was unable to leave it. She was unable to discuss her concerns with the therapist and felt at a loss as to how to move forward. At the point of narrating her story, she felt disillusioned about the therapist and the therapy, as well as counselling in general. In her view, the situation was 'a real morass . . . it's so much more complex than I'd actually imagined'.

Rachel's experiences convey fundamental fears about safety and security and show how the overlapping roles are undermining the therapy work and relationship. Her concerns about her 'child inside' suggest she was feeling very vulnerable in the situation and might revert to childlike thinking and behaving when confronted by what she saw as an unsafe relationship. Rachel's case is illustrative of other cases where the client had a damaging relationship experience. Commonly, the client withheld most of their emotional and psychological reactions from the therapist. At the same time, these clients seemed to be in relationships with therapists who did not review or check the client's understanding or experience of the situation.

The clients saw it as incumbent on the therapist, in their capacity as the practitioner in the relationship (irrespective of the role(s) they happened to be enacting), to monitor the relationship processes. Undeniably, the emotional trauma and damage experienced by Rachel and clients who had similar reactions raises serious ethical concerns and questions about the dual relationships in which they were involved, and questions about how best to address what the client perceives and experiences as damaging therapy. One client progressed from one abusive therapy relationship to another, ending up caught in an abusive cycle of dual relationships.

Eve

Being in a friendship with her former therapist is a beneficial experience for Eve, herself a therapist. Following the end of their longer-term therapy relationship, they struck up a friendship that has been ongoing for over three years. The friendship has been a good experience, although she believes this would not be the case if they had become friends before the therapy ended. Nevertheless, while therapy was ongoing, she did pursue the possibility of friendship which was refused on the grounds that it would interfere with the work and benefits of the therapy.

In retrospect, Eve believes this was the right decision, although at the time she could not see this. She believed that her therapist's handling of the therapy relationship, as well as the transition period beyond therapy towards friendship, contributed to the success of their post-therapy friendship. Eve felt that the therapist was supportive and considerate in the transition from therapy to friends and encouraged a mutual processing of the developing relationship and a redressing of the imbalance between the information known about one another. One challenge for Eve during the transition phase was an initial concern about how to introduce Jemima to family and friends. Yet, the bond between them seemed important and strong enough to both survive and sustain them in their transit to friendship. Eve believed that they both benefited from and enjoyed the post-therapy relationship; theoretically, they were similarly oriented therapists and personally and professionally had a great deal in common. Eve noted how:

if my counsellor had not later become my friend, I probably
would not have been able to understand my transferences and
projections . . . my experience has been so fruitful and enjoy-
able for me because the work I did as client was so open . . . we
both know what it is to be integrated . . . I think, feel and
know that it is not right to have an ongoing relationship . . . I
remember trying to meet Jemima as a person and said 'if I am
this circle and you are that circle, can't we meet where we
overlap' . . . (she) explained quite clearly that that would have
to be agreed, spelt out clearly, negotiated and would mean the
end of counselling. I declined! And I have only remembered
this in writing now.

Significantly, Eve's insights and understandings of the relationship process are retrospective. Over the course of the therapy Eve
wrote extensively about her experiences and perceptions, through
poetry and prose. Because of this, she was able to trace her emotional process through the relationship. Not only was she able to
do this for herself, she also felt she had a therapist who encouraged
her to reflect upon her experiences of herself and the relationship.
Her initial resentment and anger about the therapist's refusal to
become friends during the life of the therapy relationship gave way
to a conviction that the friendship would have been unmanageable
if it had begun the therapy. Eve found she was able to redeem her
projections and transference material through the friendship. While
the notion of 'redemption' conjures potent thoughts or images that
may, for some individuals, have religious associations, it was clear
from the details of her story that for her, it was an epic, intimate
and spiritual journey from 'client' to 'friend'. Thus the experience
of redeeming her 'self' in the process was transformative and life-
enhancing.
    Eve seemed able to work through the transition from therapy to
friendship, perhaps due to the deep and mutual affection in their
relationship. Not only did the dual relationship partners value one
another, they appeared to have common interests. Moreover, in
her role as client, Eve seemed well motivated, as evidenced in her
passion to learn more about herself and her friend-therapist. In this
and other successful dual relationship cases, the depth of the relational bond might constitute an important characteristic of the
transition from therapy relationship to friendship.

KEY FEATURES OF THE CLIENT EXPERIENCE OF BEING IN A DUAL RELATIONSHIP

A safe space

For some clients, representations of safety were located externally, in the guise of the therapist, while others created an internal sense of safety by emotionally withdrawing in the relationship. Those who looked for safety in the therapist tended to need a space they could trust in which to do their relational work. On the other hand, of those who located it within, some were able to sustain themselves in the relationship, while others were anxious and fearful of placing their trust in the therapist.

Several clients communicated a need to feel safe and held in the relationship, yet all of them conveyed the importance of the quality of the client–therapist relationship and its influence on the overall experience. In some cases, the complex dual or multiple relationships compromised a client's sense of safety and trust in the therapist. One spoke of needing to feel safe enough to be able to regress, yet at an intuitive level she felt that her therapist, whom she also met in training contexts, was not safe. Another had critical criteria that had to be met before she could feel safe. Primarily, she needed to be able to have a sense of whether the therapist was 'big enough and safe enough to hold me'. Having met the therapist in a non-therapy context, she felt able to assess whether they might feel safe enough in a therapy setting. Other clients needed the chance to process the various roles involved in the relationship, but found it difficult if not given the chance to do so by the therapist. In order to remain 'safe', several clients communicated how they withheld their emotional reactions and psychological processes from the therapist in the context of both the therapy relationship and the overlapping roles.

Distrust, shame, fear and anxiety about the impact and consequences of speaking out their feelings about the relationship became a potent silencer, making the situation feel increasingly unsafe. Distrust was common:

- 'I had trusted him . . . had felt safe at the beginning . . . and became increasingly mistrustful of him'
- 'I don't trust her'

- 'I'm less trusting now'
- 'I have to be able to trust their professionalism, sensitivity and ability'
- 'trust is now broken'
- 'how can I trust someone again?'

Conveying the significance and enormity of needing to feel safe in the relationship, one client spoke of her vigilant watchfulness of a previous therapist, whom she came to see as unsafe. Because of childhood trauma, she needed someone she could trust to support her safely. The next therapist with whom she had the dual relationship felt very different and she felt safe enough with them to work through some of the emotional and psychological healing she was seeking. Before becoming a client, she met her future therapist in a training and workshop context. From her observations and impressions of the therapist–trainer, she decided she could trust her enough to approach her for therapy.

In several cases, clients seemed able to sustain themselves throughout various role changes and associated boundary issues. This is not to say that they were unproblematic, but that the relational benefits counterbalanced the role conflicts and challenges. Those who successfully negotiated the tricky terrain of the dual or multiple roles did so because of their capacity to assert themselves in the relationship.This might occur by chance, since few clients seemed to have received clear information from the therapist or support from them to query the therapist's actions and decisions, or even help to identify ways of dealing with the complexities and concerns of the relationship and associated situations.

Being special

Being special was a theme in several client stories. They spoke about feeling 'special' or having been 'singled out' by their dual relationship partner. For example, a therapist might choose the client over and above other trainees or peers say, where the partners had contact in a group context. Paradoxically, as the relationship progressed over time, the client might feel paranoid in the same situation. To be special usually meant that the client complied with whatever the therapist did or wanted. Communicating the seductive power of feeling special, one client commented that:

at the time, as the client, I was so engulfed in the relationship, delighted that my tutor took such a special interest in me, I was delighted to be so special . . . I was already in a relationship where I had a positive teacher transference.

Common to those who felt special was a sense of secrecy about the relationship and an impression that they could not disclose it to others. However, the feeling of being special could change over the progression and course of the relationship, so that, for example, the client might begin feeling special but end feeling betrayed and abused.

The presenting past

For some clients the dual relationship appeared to access primal emotions, transporting them back to childhood experiences with significant others. I use the term primal here to refer to previously unacknowledged, unexplored or unresolved relational material. Some individuals made clear links between childhood relationships with significant others and their experience of relating in the dual relationship. For some, the prospect of losing the therapist and the dual relationship was traumatic, despite the fact that the relationship was difficult. Their fear of losing the therapist was associated with the loss of significant others in either the recent or distant past and fear of further loss led some to seek ongoing contact.

The impact of significant others on the client's capacity in the relationship, as well as their way of relating to the dual relationship partner, seemed important in several cases. For example, one client was raised in a large family and referred to feeling constantly 'pushed out' or 'put down' by the others, as well as having to put up with 'hand me downs' from brothers and sisters. In later years, she found herself 'pushed out' again in the dual relationship situation, whereby she had one-to-one therapy, couple therapy and group therapy, as well as supervision, with the same therapist. Although not all the roles were concurrent, there were always two roles occurring simultaneously. She felt singled out in the group context as someone who was awkward and did not fit with the other individuals. She also believed that the therapist was not skilled enough to help her and suspected they had their own unresolved psychological issues that interfered with the dual relationship.

Role issues

Even in the positive and beneficial dual relationships, some clients encountered varying degrees of uncertainty about role obligations and expectations. Ambiguity increased where informed and mutual contracting between 'client' and 'therapist' did not occur. Several clients felt guilty or shameful when they could not deal with their role confusion. Some felt angry with the therapist for not helping them to deal with the situation and their responses, yet when questioning their therapist, it usually brought the retort that they were paranoid or that 'the therapist knew best'. Where a client's confusion and conflict were matched with an unsupportive or abusive therapist, stress and anxiety increased.

It was common not to know 'how to be' either in relation to the therapist, or in the overlapping roles. Questions of role identity (that is, 'what is this role?'), self-identity in the relationship and its roles (that is, 'who am I in it?') and matters of how to enter into the role (that is, 'how can I be and behave in it?') were common in the client-contributor accounts. These questions remained difficult to resolve unless the client had a supportive or facilitative therapist to help them discuss and deal with the issues. In the majority of cases, it was evident that dealing with the confused or blurred role identity was problematic, irrespective of the quality of the relationship. Even clients who reported a beneficial dual relationship could encounter difficult periods or times of ambivalence and ambiguity over the course of the relationship. Where individuals were involved in complex multiple role situations, uncertainty increased.

A client's anxiety and ambiguity about the different role responsibilities could result in their feeling responsible for their therapist:

> there's a responsibility for me in the sense of how much do I want to shake her foundation and make her question her own self and practice, because maybe she would have to if I really challenged her . . . I feel that my awareness of all this and the complexity of it, is one-sided, so I feel it would then be in my hands, I would be doing the awareness raising.

In several cases, the client felt that the therapist, by virtue of their professional status and associated responsibilities, should support them to deal with and understand the relationship situation and the implications of the overlapping roles on their obligations to one another. As one noted, 'I had not developed the confidence or experience and skills needed for self-assertion and confrontation in adult life'. However, some could distinguish the roles and were clear about their identity in each one. One client felt especially clear about her boundaries and sense of self in the relationship and wanted a 'transparent therapist' not a blank screen, therefore meeting the therapist in social contexts was a welcome experience.

The context in which a dual relationship occurred influenced the client's perception and experience of the relationship roles. For example, where a client and therapist shared a community, knowing how to deal with the overlapping connections and the commonly held contacts was challenging and could lead to conflict and stress. In one case, the client was involved in a dual relationship with her pastor, as were other members of the pastoral community. A form of 'sibling rivalry' spread among these client-parishioners. Yet the individuals concerned were committed to making the various friendship and social relationships work so found that, with effort, the tension and conflict could be contained. This client had no regrets about the opportunity to relate to her therapist in a number of roles and felt it enriched their contact across their shared friendship, parishioner and therapy roles. Paradoxically, however, she believed that she would not knowingly enter into a similar relationship in the future because of the emotional intensity, time and energy it took to redeem relational difficulties in the overlapping roles.

Also significant was the ordering or placing of roles. Where they were concurrent, such as cases where the client was in a therapy relationship while at the same time in business, friendship or social roles with their therapist, then any clear idea about the expectations and obligations of each role was rarely evident in the client's narrative. Even in the beneficial relationships, there was recognition that a dual relationship that occurred in the context of a concurrent therapy and non-therapy role (such as, for instance, friendship) was particularly difficult. Two notable exceptions to this were clients who were able to separate out the various roles and manage the boundary transitions between therapy and non-therapy contexts.

At the time of their contribution to the research, all of the clients were themselves trained therapists, so were familiar with the therapeutic notion of 'boundary' and appeared to have their own understanding and interpretation of the term when recounting their story. At the time of the dual relationship, however, many of the clients were trainees and did not fully comprehend the boundaries between therapy and non-therapy contact.

Generally, those who found the dual relationship most harmful or debilitating found the overlapping roles most difficult to deal with. Some would psychologically 'switch off' in order not to feel their emotional and psychological reactions and thus help themselves deal with the situation and maintain an impression of safety. This usually meant that they were emotionally unavailable in the relationship, often remaining silent, or pretending that they were fine.

Occasions when a client was able to move in and between roles more comfortably or competently seemed to be characterized by the matching of a supportive therapist with a client who appeared aware of the relationship roles and their part in constructing them. These clients appeared more psychologically robust and able to sustain themselves in the various roles. One client found that overlapping therapy and non-therapy contact actually enriched her experience of both. Moving between client, trainee and social roles was not difficult for her because she felt able to hold the boundaries between roles. This client was able to sustain herself in some way in the roles. This ability and experience was not, however, common in the client group. A different, yet similarly positive experience was communicated by another client who believed she benefited from having a therapist who was able to hold firm boundaries: 'a very firm frame . . . is another thing which makes it possible to express whatever I'm feeling'. This client was in analytical therapy and encountered her analyst at professional meetings. She believed this overlap was manageable because of the clear boundaries and frame around the therapy relationship.

Transitions between concurrent roles were most challenging for those struggling to make sense of the relationship. One client recognized she had difficulty, yet also knew she simply could not say 'no' to her therapist when they asked her to meet them in a social role. She found it awkward, hating it at the time, but paradoxically, was unable to extract herself. It felt as though the therapist was doing her a favour. This exerted a major emotional hold on the client that was complicated by the fact that this relationship had featured significantly in a great part of her adult life, thus she felt she could not refuse her. The therapist became a key person, associated with a significant parental figure; so much so, that the loss of the relationship would have been traumatic. Her emotional pull to stay in the relationship constituted a 'see-sawing' of emotions echoed in several cases.

For those clients who felt they had roles forced upon them, the experience was frustrating yet typified by their reluctance or inability to challenge the situation. Reluctance related to fear of the therapist, as well as fear of the consequences of a challenge from them. One client in a multiple role relationship noted that her therapist 'insisted I participate in one of his weekly therapy groups'. Another spoke of how additional roles, or changes in the roles, were *ad hoc* and not discussed with her, nevertheless 'the pull was . . . this would be good and all the rest of it'. These transitions appeared to occur without any attempt by the therapist to help the client understand the relational changes. Having the therapist claim that the extra roles were for the client's benefit was difficult to reconcile with how she felt about the situation.

Autonomy and consent

Although a client might appear to consent to participate, they might not fully comprehend the potential consequences of the changing roles:

> My therapist was actually a (fellow) student on the course . . . she'd said she might see me from time to time around the place, would this be a problem, and I said no and I think one of the reasons I said no was that I didn't understand the intensity of the relationship that could develop between therapist and client . . . which was a reflection of where I was at the time . . . I wasn't good at understanding the intensity of any sort of relationship really.

Explicit informed and willing consent to participate in the dual or multiple role relationship was evident in only a few stories. Several clients felt that their therapist assumed their consent. Few entered the relationship aware of the potential implications and challenges and it was only in retrospect that the complexity and seriousness of the situation became evident. Some commented about how it took years to process the harmful impact of the relationship. One became so engrossed in the relationship and experience of being special, that she only later realized she had not given informed consent at the outset. Usually, the transition from a sole role to dual or multiple roles was not consensual on the clients' part. As one client stated, 'I did not understand the process . . . and did not read anything untoward into the duality'.

Several clients appeared to give consent to take on additional roles, yet privately felt unhappy or confused about the new role. For example, one client saw her livelihood and career as dependent on being compliant and willing to take on additional roles with her former therapist. There was an inextricable link between her livelihood and the relationship with her former therapist. The dual relationship partner appeared to exert a powerful influence over her ability to disclose the relationship to others. A key factor for her was a sense of shame at the prospect of colleagues discovering how things had been in the dual relationship. To speak the unspeakable was too shameful and daunting.

At the time of the dual relationship, this client was a fellow student of her therapist and felt she was naïve about relationship dynamics, although she wondered if things might have been different if she had been further into her training, or more aware in relationships. Another felt that her therapist assumed too much about her experience and understanding of the relationship and consequently failed to encourage her to voice her issues or concerns. She wondered whether the therapist's theoretical orientation (humanistic, person-centred) placed too much responsibility onto the client and assumed too much about her capacity to respond, as well as to sustain herself in the relationship.

For one client, although seeing her therapist criticised at professional meetings was difficult to deal with, she also found that the collegial contact gave her additional insight into him as a person. Over time, they became more like siblings than client and therapist or colleagues. At the time of the research interview, their relationship had gone through further transitions to the point where they were no longer in a therapy relationship and were moving into becoming co-students on a training course. This client seemed able to bring her knowledge, relational experience and wisdom into the dual relationship situation. However, few clients were so clear about their dual relationship and the relational complexities that arose from it, or so apparently able to deal with the role conflict.

Confidentiality

Several clients thought confidentiality was crucial. One spoke of how it was central to the success of the dual relationship. She and her dual relationship partner encountered one another frequently at business meetings, so she needed to know that her personal processes disclosed in a therapy setting would not leach into the context of the professional association. Another spoke of the distress of having her private disclosures publicized in a training group context. Both clients valued confidentiality. One was able to secure a respectful contract about confidentiality with their therapist, while the other found the therapist disrespectful and unwilling to uphold her confidences disclosed in therapy. For the latter client, the unauthorized disclosures were tantamount to abuse and made the training group seem extremely unsafe. Paradoxically, at the same time she felt trapped, unable to escape the group. She felt scapegoated and bullied and became increasingly vulnerable and unable to challenge the therapist's behaviour. In what became a vicious circle, distrust led to further withholding of information, feelings and communication, and so on, in a negative spiral of emotions.

Power dynamics in the relationship roles

Role and relational power appeared to be a central issue in all the relationships, with responsibilities and obligations associated with any given relationship role becoming a key feature. First contact with the therapist was usually in the role of 'client', thus the primary relationship was a therapy one. Inherent power inequities, as well as naïve hope, may have influenced a client's capacity to assess whether or not the dual relationship was really in their own best interests. Knowledge about how dual relationships begin raises questions about decisions taken in the relationships' early stages – especially in relation to the role the client takes in these. Whether a role transition is intentional or circumstantial, it is significant with regard to the distribution of relational power. Several clients seemed to be completely unprepared for the full impact of moving between dual and multi-roles and felt disempowered by the process.

These clients tended to feel obliged to take up the role, yet at the same time, felt uncertain about how and where to place their priority or allegiance in the various relationship roles. In some cases, this concern or angst about positioning themselves in the roles generated stress.

Few clients moved between roles with ease. Those who did move more freely tended to be assertive and clear about the purpose and limits of the roles, as well as have a supportive dual relationship partner. Clients who encountered difficulties tended to have an unsupportive therapist. Perhaps a 'good fit' might be dual relationship partners who can reflexively and reflectively relate throughout their shared roles. Essentially, clients appeared to have difficulty knowing how to be in the relationship and its roles. The boundaries between roles were often difficult to 'see'. Given that the client-contributors were themselves therapists (at the time of recounting their story in the research interview context) with some understanding of the concept of relationship boundaries, it suggests that the situation for those clients without this knowledge or experience is tricky.

Robustness in the relationship roles

Some clients were seemingly less robust, apparently in relationships with therapists who did not support them or provide conditions for a more productive or satisfying relationship. Questions of whether a client is sufficiently robust to withstand a dual relationship most obviously arose in the debilitating or damaging cases. Essentially, in these cases the client seemed unable to say 'no' to the therapist and could not assert their rights or responsibilities in the relationship. Most often, there was no clear sense of their relational responsibilities – either what they were or how to fulfil them. Conversely, clients who survived and benefited from the experience, and who appeared to have been left positively and emotionally 'intact' from the experience, communicated a number of different core experiences and personal qualities and characteristics in their stories. When the clients' experiences of dual relationships tended towards the positive, they were more likely to be sharing their thoughts or emotions with their therapist, or explaining how they experienced the situation, so that the therapist understood how they felt. In addition they were often involved in mutually negotiating the progress of the relationship.

When clients encountered difficulty being in a dual relationship they appeared to:
- have difficulty negotiating the various roles;
- have difficulty sustaining self in the various relationship roles;
- experience conflict between the demands or expectations (self-imposed perceived or imposed externally through culturally, socially or professionally influences) of the relationship roles and their own impressions and experiences in the situation;
- feel unsupported by the therapist;
- have difficulty in articulating their concerns or problems (to self, the therapist, or anyone else);
- feel trapped in the relationship;
- fear losing the relationship and thus be unable to withdraw or challenge the therapist;
- have a negative impression of the therapist.

When clients found being in a dual relationship a positive experience they appeared to have a capacity for:
- assertiveness;
- self-confidence;
- comprehending the relational situation and process;
- assessing their therapist's skills, qualities and abilities to provide them with a good enough therapy relationship;
- articulating their experiences and perceptions;
- self-disclosure;
- mutual and collaborative relations with the therapist;
- inner, psychological resources to support them in the relationship;
- a positive attachment to the therapist.

Arguably, if a client is not sufficiently robust, we need to question the validity and integrity of forming a dual relationship and the client's capacity for relational responsibility. If the client is not robust and the relationship is unavoidable, extreme care is probably required, along with good supervision and appropriate client consultation. In such cases, it might be that minimal, non-intimate contact is a preferred limit in order to support the client to identify the different relational roles and help them to differentiate and process their experiences in a supportive therapy context. This, arguably, suggests the need for necessary relational conditions for client safety and more beneficial relationship outcomes.

The client experiences and perceptions both support and refute existing thinking and practice. They confirm that they can be harmful (Pope and Vasquez, 1998) but refute claims that all dual relationships are damaging or inadvisable by supporting the anecdotes and rhetoric that some can actually be beneficial (Clarkson, 1994; Lazarus and Zur, 2002; McLeod, 1998; Syme, 2003; Tudor, 2000). Strikingly, in some cases a dual relationship was a deeply rewarding experience. Equally, however, we cannot ignore the potent evidence that they were harmful, reflecting reports on the type of emotional and psychological damage encountered in sexual dual relationships (see, for example, Pope, 1988a; Russell, 1993). With sharp clarity, the clients' and practitioners' experiences show how dual relationships can elicit concerns and difficulties around being in role, our robustness in them and how as practitioners we manage (or mismanage) our relational ethics. What they also show is the extreme nature of the emotional roller-coaster that some clients encounter. A further key finding that the literature largely ignores is the fact that therapists can also experience harm. It is this variability, however, that makes it impossible to offer definitive statements regarding 'what dual relationships work best with whom and in what context', since it is clear that client and therapist dual relationships constitute complex, potent and diverse relational 'events'.

Similar to Rennie's (1994a, 1994b) findings on client reflexivity and deference, some client contributors showed how, at times, they withhold reactions and defer to their therapist. All too often, in fact, a client's response was compliance and silence. If we note how some client-contributors withheld their thoughts from their therapist, as well as the evidence that some therapists withheld their experience and thoughts from peers and supervisors, then encouraging individuals to speak out seems appropriate and necessary. That said, perhaps we should not be too surprised that the ebb and flow of dual relationships can be chaotic and conflicted and that we do not speak about our resulting distress.

What prospect is there for the client who enters into a dual or multiple role relationship with an inexperienced, inept or abusive practitioner? Some clients clearly encountered role confusion and stress in their experiences of dual and multiple role relationships. When a client is confused or emotionally vulnerable, it is hardly surprising that they might naïvely assume or hope that the therapist knows best and will offer them a place of safety. Given that when a client presents for therapy they are encountering some kind of personal or relational issue, we can reasonably assume that this might influence their capacity to be in role, as well as make decisions in that role. Where the practitioner abuses this trust, the consequences can evidently be traumatic and harrowing. Clients who had a bad experience seemed to find it difficult to sustain self emotionally (encountering difficulties managing or mediating their various feelings) or psychologically (experiencing problems reflecting on or making reasoned decisions). It is evident that some clients, for whatever reason, have difficulty assessing what is right or wrong in the relationship. Disturbingly, in some cases, individuals appeared to enter dual or multiple roles intuitively or with little critical reflection. In spite of these difficult and harmful dual relationship experiences, we need to remember that several clients did find the relationship beneficial and rewarding.

Chapter 9

Practitioner experiences of being in non-sexual dual and multiple role relationships

What's the big deal [about dual relationships]? Are we, by sanctifying the privacy, secrecy and whatever of the therapeutic relationship, are we in some way implying that what's going to happen there is so shameful it needs to be kept out of the public eye, that it's going to be so weird that it can't possibly mix with anything else? You could end up being incredibly precious about it and unnecessarily so.

(A practitioner-contributor)

A PRAGMATIC PROCESS

Whereas the client experience tended to be an emotional one, by contrast, the practitioner experience was more of an intellectual, pragmatic process. The practitioners' experiences and ways of being in dual or multiple roles were evident in two key ways. First, they encountered issues identifying the limits and obligations of roles and experienced difficulties moving between the roles. Secondly, they faced challenges and problems associated with role confidentiality. In particular, in organizational contexts, difficulties arose around communications between the therapist and colleagues, managers or others with an interest or stake in the client's well-being. Additionally, many of the therapists experienced conflicts related to limits and lines of confidentiality, the stress of managing requests from management for information about the client, and tensions between the roles where there were varying or conflicting role expectations and responsibilities. For those who worked in primary care, managed care or similar NHS contexts, overlapping roles were unavoidable. In relation to dealing with such complex relational situations, one therapist aptly captured the thoughts of many others when she said it was like moving in 'uncharted territory, the kind that ordinarily I would be very concerned about'.

Several individuals conveyed an image of competence and confidence when recounting their dual relationship experience. Experienced practitioners, accustomed to dealing with complex relational situations, as well as managing the challenges of ethical and moral problem-solving, they appeared comfortable when talking about their abilities in the relationship. In addition, they were open to expressing their strengths and limitations and how they might influence the dual relationship. For others, however, the emotional impact of the dual relationship seemed difficult to acknowledge and in some contexts, it seemed preferable to mask problems or perceived weaknesses. For example, individuals working within organizational settings felt compromised by the competing role demands of organization and relationship, with some choosing to minimize or mask their concerns in order to avoid colleagues and managers regarding them as ineffective or unethical.

KEY FEATURES OF THE PRACTITIONER EXPERIENCE

Role identity and obligations

All therapists experienced role-related issues or concerns, irrespective of whether the overall relationship experience was beneficial, damaging or a combination of both. It was clear that several therapists believed their role carried explicit and implicit ethical and moral obligations. They saw this as a crucial part of their participation and responsibility in the relationship. However, several others criticised the client for not taking responsibility in the day-to-day lived experiences of the dual relationship. This occurred across a range of theoretical perspectives from psychoanalytical to humanistic.

Where the therapist's relationship with the client involved relating through multiple roles and contexts, the experience was challenging and sometimes stressful. For those working and relating to clients in an organizational or primary care context, role identity and the limits of roles shared with the client were often unclear. Especially problematic were cases where the therapist's manager(s) appeared not to understand, recognize or promote client autonomy, or the need for a client to consent to have details of their work with the therapist-cum-worker disclosed to a third party. Several therapists believed this type of situation was fuelled by management paranoia and fears that staff, in their client role and context, were talking about or criticising them. While on one hand management culture was concerned about rapidly resolving staff concerns in order to get on with their work, by contrast, the counselling culture was more about protecting clients' well-being, anonymity and confidentiality.

Several practitioners believed that management misunderstood what counselling was about. Characteristic of this was conflict between the organizational culture and the dynamics and aims of therapy, which often occurred when the practitioner's theoretical orientation conflicted with the organizational aims and practices. In particular, those who worked with clients in a primary care, case-managed or secure care context were challenged when confronted by colleagues and an organizational culture that did not understand or recognize the role, values or purpose of the therapy relationship they were offering. For two therapists who experienced dual relationships in secure care contexts, issues arose around the conflict between a 'capture and cure' ethic and the apparently libertarian values of counselling and psychotherapy that espoused client autonomy and a duty of care. Colleagues challenged their clinical and theoretical orientation and preferences when they belittled the work or, as in one case, attempted to sabotage it by claiming that no therapy rooms were available, or that the client could not be located.

Ambiguous role identity or ambivalence about role obligations could generate stress. Conversely, individuals experienced less stress when they were relatively clear about their roles. In a few cases, a practitioner's need to secure a training placement had influenced the development of a dual relationship, resulting in conflict and stress between training placement requirements and obligations to the client.

Role boundaries

Most therapist-contributors encountered boundary challenges and struggles as part of the experience of being in a dual relationship. Particularly challenging were issues around identifying role and boundary limits. One practitioner spoke of the difficulty and stress of attempting to remember the limits of the roles she shared with clients. Where she was trainer, counsellor and supervisor to several clients, she faced an onerous task remembering how to greet them outside the therapy context. Eventually, she decided that the stress of managing this outweighed any benefits and decided not to enter into further dual relationships.

One practitioner had a positive opinion of blurred boundaries and believed that 'in some respects the boundaries are quite blurred between friendship and counselling', communicating a congruent and transparent way of being that she upheld irrespective of the role. She spoke of a core set of human communication skills and attitudes that wove their way through all her interpersonal connections. Her approach was consistent, whether in the role of therapist, colleague or friend and aligned with a humanistic, person-centred orientation. Provided she and the other person were clear about their limits of confidentiality, it was possible to relate through a number of different roles. For this person, the situation was less 'being in role' and more 'person in relationship'. Another practitioner chose not to discuss the overlapping therapy and peer development group roles that she shared with her client because 'it kept the thing separate, we didn't talk about the group stuff in the therapy and we didn't talk about the therapy stuff in the group'. She assumed that the client could deal with remaining silent about the relationship roles.

While for some therapists this approach was both preferable and manageable, for others, clearly delineated boundaries and role markers were essential. For example, some of the psychodynamic practitioners would not enter into a dual relationship with a current client, but would consider it beyond the ending of the therapy relationship. One spoke of giving the client the opportunity to resolve transference issues or psychological projections. In her view, unless this occurred, a dual relationship was inadvisable. Carol's experience of working with dual and multiple role relationships challenged her capacity to manage the tensions and challenges of relationship boundaries. Her situation captures that of several others in organizational or multiple role relationship settings.

Carol

Carol had a varied experience of juggling multiple role relationships with her clients. Working in private practice, as well as in the voluntary sector, Carol specialized in advocacy and working with disaffected people. She found it challenging to balance collegial, facilitator, advocate and therapy roles with clients and

> trying to provide, having to provide, all . . . kinds of support . . . it's not so much duality . . . it's the lack of other support . . . I persuaded her to come and stay with me without thinking she would actually turn up, but she did . . . I knew she couldn't go back, so I then became not only group facilitator, but rescue worker . . . I was in a dual role in trying . . . to provide social support for her . . . and actually I was counselling her as well . . . so I went through a period of being both counsellor and advocate . . . the specialist knowledge you have . . . makes you much more effective as an advocate for that person.

Carol believed that suitable support or knowledge was not available locally, therefore she felt obliged to take on advocacy tasks alongside a concurrent therapy role. For her, the perception that other suitable professional support was unavailable meant that she felt pressured to take on certain non-therapy tasks and functions for her clients. She believed that combining therapy and advocacy roles was both necessary and possible:

> the counsellor would be a good advocate . . . you know more about the person than anybody else . . . you're in the position to make the best case and actually in the sense of getting them to stand up for themselves, to actually advocate for themselves, that's actually part of the getting well process I think.

For Carol this way of being with her client demonstrated helpful actions. Effectively, she saw the different roles as opportunities for modelling and learning, making it possible for the client to develop interpersonal and conflict resolution skills by witnessing these in their work together. For Carol, this represented duality at its best. The situation was not particularly problematic, yet it was stressful. The stresses appeared to have taken their toll, as her tearful response when she had finished recounting her situation suggested. Carol's experience captures the conviction held by several therapist-contributors that we need to view the role of practitioner in a dual or multiple role relationship within the context of changing practices and demands in the helping professions. The vagaries and idiosyncracies of a rapidly evolving counselling field raised many questions and concerns about the identity and obligations of the counsellor's role.

Confidentiality

In organizational contexts, individuals felt compromised about boundaries of confidentiality, despite their aim to uphold the client's rights to a confidential relationship. However, this was not exclusive to organizational contexts, since those who worked in rural or small town settings faced similar challenges. Within the setting of private practice in a rural community, one practitioner spoke of conflicts and challenges faced when clients were also in social contact with her friends. One way of managing the relational boundaries involved agreeing limits of confidentiality with the client, as well as with her friends and 'we didn't deal with anything connected with the mutual friendship'. This demanded that she was constantly attentive to the overlapping relationships in her local community. Additionally, she was concerned about the impact of 'splitting-off' mutual friends as topics in the therapy relationship. Beyond the completion of their therapy work, the client went into counselling with another counsellor, presumably to work on issues that were taboo in their therapy work and relationship.

Concerns about confidentiality appeared to be closely associated with the context in which the relationship occurred and the way in which the setting affected confidentiality. For example, the nine practitioners who worked in organizational settings referred to difficulties and conflicts associated with confidentiality. Several other therapists also referred to the challenges of managing confidentiality and anonymity in a rural community context. In an organizational context, it was difficult to manage the limits of confidentiality between what occurred in the confines of the one-to-one therapy work and what happened outside the therapy room and contract. Where a therapist had a multi-role job in the organization, overlapping connections with a client's line manager could be problematic. As one therapist noted:

> the difficulty for me was . . . not to take his interpretations out of the room with me, because I then had to leave our sessions and go to a meeting with his line manager.

According to the practitioners, managers did not seem to understand the purpose or role of the counselling service, sometimes offering or seeking information about clients. One practitioner felt that management could be paranoid about what clients might disclose in confidence. She worked in a welfare role within a large organization and spoke about how managers attempt to offer unnecessary information about clients and the impact this has on her:

> the guilty knowledge that we have is tremendous because every manager will come up to you about the member of his or her staff and tell you things that they believe you need to know . . . they ignore that you're counselling [the client] . . . as far as they're concerned they are giving background information to the welfare manager.

According to one therapist, dealing with confidentiality conflicts demanded a 'balancing act that can . . . be quite a difficult thing to do. [A]sking . . . what is it that we can take out that is safe to use and can be more generally known?' Balancing what can/cannot be disclosed was especially challenging for one therapist employed in a multidisciplinary primary healthcare context. He faced daily decisions related to managing staff inquisitiveness about the therapy work he offered to one of the clients. Group and interpersonal staff dynamics made it especially important that he hold the boundaries between what was private and what was public. Therapy in his work context was innovative and thus both interesting and suspect to other staff members. This was mirrored for one of the two therapists who worked in a secure care context. Organizational culture and opposition to what was perceived as an unnecessary one-to-one relationship with an inmate made it difficult to protect client confidentiality. Because of the secure setting, the location of the therapy sessions needed to be known and often these were not conducive to confidential work. The other therapist working in a secure context found that upholding confidentiality was challenging but possible, provided clear contracting occurred between her and the clients whom she encountered in other staff or inmate contexts.

Many of the therapists' role-related issues or conflicts were associated with confidentiality issues specific to the relationship context. In particular, there were issues of defining limits and boundaries of confidentiality in workplace dual relationships. In addition, there were concerns about a clash between the needs and aims of the organization and the therapist's desire to uphold client needs for confidentiality. Theory and ethics codes were useful, but for those living and working in rural or small community contexts, their scope did not account for the complexities of the situation.

Assessment

One therapist had her 'bottom line' measure of whether a role was appropriate or not. Essentially, where there was a current therapy relationship, social contact reduced or ceased for the duration of the therapy. Through this, she remained focused on the client's needs. If the social or friendship relationship developed beyond the end of therapy, then it was an entirely different matter. Here, she was open to a social relationship developing, depending upon the client's capacity for it, as well as the content and process of the therapy work and relationship. Her integrative theoretical and clinical approach meant that she would draw upon psychological insights into human psychology to help her assess whether or not a dual relationship was appropriate. For example, she frequently drew on psychodynamic insights, including attachment theory and notions of transference and countertransference to inform her thinking and actions. In addition, supportive yet challenging supervision and peer support group helped her to manage and monitor the relationship boundaries. Like this practitioner, others also appeared to use theory in a number of ways, including:

- to help them decide whether or not a dual relationship was appropriate;
- to assess the client's capacity to enter into a dual relationship; and
- to inform their decisions and actions over the course of the therapy relationship and across the various dual or multiple overlapping roles.

Several practitioners alluded to a *therapy frame* that supported their thinking and practice. Thirteen of the therapists practised from a position that was rooted in person-centred theory and practice, four worked from a psychodynamic stance and one from an existential perspective, yet few explicitly referred to the impact or influence of these on the dual relationship. One spoke of drawing on insights from attachment theory to help her understand the emotional and relational needs of the client. Of those who worked in organizational contexts, some found existing theory provided an inadequate account of dual relationships that occurred in these contexts.

Some referred to theory when thinking about the relationship dynamics. Psychodynamic concepts featured prominently here, including with some therapists who were principally humanistic in orientation. From an NLP (neurolinguistic programming) informed position, one practitioner noted how:

> it's a systemic approach of using the information that I gather from myself, from her, and from this position of detachment, to constantly be aware of what will be the best approaches to take at any given time.

Of those practitioners who either explicitly or tacitly communicated an understanding of a client's capacity to be in the relationship, one felt she could recognize when a dual relationship was inappropriate or unlikely to work. A person-centred practitioner, she also drew on psychodynamic insights and concepts, including attachment theory, to inform her thinking and decisions about whether or not a client could sustain other roles over and above the therapy relationship.

Emotional and spiritual bonds

Intriguingly, while role and boundary issues were prominent, the emotional realms of the dual relationship experience did not overtly feature. On rare occasions where therapists explicitly communicated their emotional responses and attachment to the relationship, they seemed to do so for a variety of reasons. These included: blaming self for an unpleasant relationship outcome; feeling ashamed about how they handled overlapping roles; and conveying the stress and anxiety associated with relationships that occurred in complex contexts. Therapist stories tended to convey the complications and challenges of managing dual and multiple overlapping roles rather than the relational dynamics.

However, in a few cases the practitioner communicated the pleasures and potentialities of the dual relationship. One noted that:

> because we care about each other so much, because we are in the business that we are (personal and professional development), we have to be even more watchful of each other's boundaries, each other's support . . . it's absolutely critically important and yet at the same time loving and caring.

Although explicit references to an emotional bond were rare, an intense and intimate bond existed between some dual relationship partners. There were instances of a deeply felt, intuitive bond between them. One therapist realized the depth and significance of the bond between herself and her dual relationship partner and spoke of it as a resonance that needed no words, but simply existed. There seemed to be an intimacy in the relationship that was of a deeply spiritual rather than a sexual nature.

Some therapists clearly valued the relationship, speaking of roles that appeared to be mutually constructed. Over time, the practice of negotiating roles appeared to bring about an easy familiarity. Significantly, the more self-aware and confident they were (as both a person and practitioner) the more successfully they facilitated the dual relationship. They communicated a commitment to ongoing personal and professional development, with a self-questioning attitude that seemed to allow them to extend the same to their client/dual relationship partner.

Nevertheless, few practitioners explicitly communicated emotional reactions or attachments to their dual relationship partners or the relationship situation. Perhaps job or work-related stress is more acceptable to admit to than deeper emotional distress, anxiety or intimate bonding. Alternatively, it might suggest that therapists who contributed to the research were largely those who did not encounter relational stress, ambiguity or conflict. Equally, perhaps some were able to put themselves forward, risking shame or embarrassment in the researcher–contributor relationship.

Supervision

At least half of the practitioners did not refer to the role or influence of supervision in their experience, management or monitoring of the dual relationship. Supervision of the dual relationships appeared to be problematic for several therapists who did comment on supervisory matters in relation to their dual relationship. Responses included inhibitions or concerns. The prospect of disclosing the dual relationship generated shame or guilt. In addition, some doubted the supervisor's ability to supervise the dual relationship situation. Some were embarrassed about experiencing problems. A few were fearful of admitting to the dual relationship, preferring to remain silent about it. Paradoxically, not being able to talk about the situation meant that the practitioners were alone in their relational difficulties, removed from the support or challenge of peer or consultative supervision. One practitioner's difficulty with disclosing the case in supervision was associated with the client's sexual attraction to them and their own anxiety about acknowledging and discussing this with anyone else. When the client attempted to draw the therapist into further social contact, the therapist became aware of the intensity of the situation. Unable to disclose their anxiety and concern in supervision, they bore the problem alone and bitterly regretted their earlier decision to have non-therapy contact with the client. It left the practitioner unwilling to enter into subsequent dual relationships.

Several communicated a form of self-supervision, suggesting a self-aware way of being in the relationship, including a capacity for critical reflexivity and a commitment to ongoing personal and professional growth. Individuals who demonstrated these qualities seemed to encourage the client into mutually processing and reviewing the content and process of the dual or multiple role relationship. With some, there were tacit agreements between themselves and the client to support clear relationship limits and boundaries.

Practitioners able to support self and client were also using peer and consultative supervision to help them monitor and manage the relationship. One counsellor involved the client in reviewing and monitoring the relationship and spoke of the need to trust the client's perceptions and interpretations of shared knowledge, people and contacts. She believed that pre-therapy social contact in a shared rural community had actually enabled the client to develop a crucial and enabling level of trust in her as a therapist. This practitioner seemed able to use her own and the client's impressions of the relationship within a type of internalized supervisory process.

Several practitioners' stories conveyed the significance of supervision in their dual relationship experience. In some cases, however, they felt the quality of supervision was unsatisfactory. For some, it signified the supervisor's inexperience or inadequacy. For the novice therapist, the potential for problems increased. In a few cases, the therapist was unable to use the supervision context to discuss dual relationships because of the anxiety, guilt or shame that they could not deal with the situation. In other cases, it was evident that the therapist recognized the limited ability of the supervisor to appropriately support and challenge them in the dual relationship.

Alison's case, shown below, captures the difficulties that can occur in relation to supervision. Significantly, her story shows how a practitioner's capacity for relational understanding can grow over time, reducing dependency on external supervision as one's internal supervisor develops.

Alison

Social and friendship contact with former clients was both positive and negative for Alison. She worked as an integrative practitioner, drawing on her early humanistic training, as well as later psycho-dynamic theoretical influences. In her early days as a novice practitioner, she entered into a short-term therapy relationship with a client that extended over ten sessions. When the client requested that they meet socially after the therapy contract ended, Alison felt unsure about what to do. She was uncertain whether to enter into social contact with the client and felt unable to take the issue to supervision, instead relying on her intuitive sense of whether the action was right or wrong, with that particular client, at that particular time in her development as a therapist. According to Alison, the client had:

> found the counselling exceptionally helpful but I don't know how far, with hindsight, how far she wanted to please me, I think there was an element of that in it and she was a very lonely woman and I liked her a lot and she did say something about 'I feel as though you've become my friend and I wish we could be friends, do you think we could meet for coffee?' . . . I was aware of discomfort around the whole thing . . . I talked it through with my supervisor and my supervisor really took the line that it was up to me.

Alison felt that the supervisor was inexperienced and unable to offer support and challenge when she most needed it:

> I realized that . . . as a relatively inexperienced counsellor I probably needed more support and guidance about it than now . . . I think that I know what the issues are now and I wouldn't expect the same kind of perhaps slightly probing or pushing me to identify how I really feel about it . . . and I think I disguised some of my negative feelings about this client . . . so maybe I wasn't able to use those bits of discomfort about her that might have been helpful . . . and I think now I would have used much more immediacy with her about my own feelings . . . I don't think [the supervisor] enabled, perhaps [she] didn't have the insight.

The conjunction of not knowing the supervisor with an impression that they lacked competence led to Alison being less open and honest about the dual relationship than she could have been. Alison was a trained and experienced therapist at the time of the research interview and was reflecting on a relationship that occurred during her time as a trainee practitioner. She felt she had learned a great deal from the experience and had since successfully formed a dual relationship with a former client. She suspected that the possibility of a dual relationship with the first client was not an appropriate option. Since she felt unable to fully take the issue to supervision, she trusted her intuitive sense that to pursue a relationship, with this particular client, would have been inappropriate, 'because I think by then it had occurred to me "well what if she wanted to come back for counselling in the future?" she would have to see somebody else whether she liked it or not'. Her ambiguity and self-questioning led her to decide not to pursue a friendship relationship with that particular client.

However, Alison's recent experience of developing a friendship with a former client portrays a different story and shows how evolving personal and professional skills and knowledge influenced her capacity to decide whether a dual relationship was appropriate. In the second dual relationship, the therapy relationship had lasted over sixty sessions and ended mutually. Alison thought the success of the relationship was partly to do with her being much more confident and competent as a practitioner and being able to recognize when it is appropriate or not to enter into such a relationship:

but I just wish I had been able to be more aware and more
honest about the whole thing both with myself, with my
supervisor and with my client from the outset and that's the
difference . . . with Sarah I talked at length about what it
would mean to be friends, we talked at length about had she
actually finished the counselling, what would happen if she
wanted to come back . . . we spent a lot of time over quite an
extended period so we didn't make up our minds about it but it
got raised that we liked each other a lot . . . she was quite
aware . . . she was a [helping professional] and I think she had
an awareness of these things . . . so we explored all those kinds
of things before we ever reached the point of saying 'ok let's
see how it goes, we might both decide that this isn't right after
all and let's be honest with each other about it' . . . one of the
things I actually had to separate was how far was our mutual
wish for this to become a friendship a kind of denial of the
attachment issues in the relationship and the detachment issues
if you like, the feelings of loss and so on that would go with the
end of the [therapy] relationship.

Alison's narrative shows how her developing confidence, knowledge and experience enabled her to approach the second dual
relationship differently. It also shows how her thinking about her
own process, the quality of the therapy relationship and the client's
capacity had progressed – to the point where she seemed able to
question the motives of pursuing a friendship with a client once the
therapy ended. Importantly, she comments on her awareness that
pursuit of duality might mask attempts to delay or deny loss of a
valuable bond between herself and the client. Clearly, these are
complex matters, but having raised them, she was able to appropriately explore them in the therapy relationship and in supervision. She believed that she had

developed more awareness of the issues . . . the first time I
experienced it . . . it was like 'oh hell what do I do now?' the
client's said this and I don't know what to do . . . whereas
when it happened subsequently, at least I had that experience
to draw on and be able to take my time about it, not feel as
though I had to say yes or no straight away . . . so I had felt
quite a lot of pressure, pressure on myself I suppose but it

appeared to be pressure from the client to say yes or no . . . I was worried about her feelings because she was insecure.

Alison's story shows how she grew personally and professionally to a point where she was able to 'process the process' and provide her own critical inner supervisor, supported by an external supervisory consultant. As an integrative practitioner, Alison drew on a number of theoretical ideas and used attachment theory to help her conceptualize the relational situation and assess whether she and the client could sustain a dual relationship. In the first dual relationship experience, she had found it difficult to deal with her ambiguity and ambivalence and seemed to have felt pressured into social contact with the client. Clearly, in such a state, when matched with a 'demanding' client, a therapist could conceivably acquiesce, reluctantly taking themselves into a dual relationship. In the second dual relationship, she was aware of how she had moved on and was now able to discriminate for herself whether a relationship was appropriate or not. She appeared to be far less anxious about the second dual relationship and was able to use her supervisor consultant as a resource. She could also rely more on her intuitive responses and check them against her theoretical and clinical preferences. In addition, she was more able to tolerate ambivalent feelings. Alison's experience suggests that the knowledge, skills and qualities of the practitioner are significant features in how a therapist might enter into and deal with a dual relationship.

Practitioners harmed in a dual relationship

Paradoxically, we usually overlook the possibility that a dual relationship can harm the practitioner. Nonetheless, cases where a client inundates the therapist with letters, visits or pleas for contact either during the therapy relationship or beyond its end (Clarkson, 1994; Clarkson and Murdin, 1996; Hedges, 1997; Tudor, 1999) are not unknown. Other instances of therapists being damaged are associated with reports of clients diagnosed with borderline personality disorder and thought to have manipulated their therapist and attempted to draw them out of the therapist role and into a 'special' relationship (Gutheil and Gabbard 1995; Smith and Fitzpatrick, 1995). This theme is taken up by Clarkson and Murdin (1996), who talk about 'victim's revenge' when referring to a client's rebuffed attempts to induce the practitioner to enter into unorthodox or unprofessional practice. An inexperienced or inept therapist might become unsuspecting prey. Critics of this line of thinking have dismissed it as an attempt to re-victimize and blame the original 'victim' (that is the client) (Gutheil and Gabbard, 1995).

For many of the practitioners, the relationship could generate conflict and anxiety. In the less positive or harmful cases, the relational experience was especially stressful. Indeed, it was in the context of role and relationship conflict that most of the emotional content of the therapist experiences was evident. In one case, the narrator became emotional and tearful when speaking of the complex and demanding nature of her multi-role work with clients. Despite the fact that she had chosen the job it was, nevertheless, difficult managing the overlapping roles with clients. One practitioner felt out of control of the situation and subject to the manipulation and control of the client. This is contrary to popular views of dual relationships, where the focus is usually on the client as victim.

Another contributor spoke of conflict and guilt when the relationship with a former client ended traumatically, with his being virtually stalked by the client. After what seemed a successful ending of the therapy, the practitioner accepted the former client's invitation to a social event, but regretted what followed. The client showered him with gifts and requests for further contact and he became aware of the possibility of their making sexual overtures. The notion of being drawn or seduced into a relationship, was commented on by one practitioner:

> maybe she wanted to please me and . . . somehow pay me back for the help I had given her. I don't think I had any awareness that that might be an issue . . . I became increasingly aware . . . that this was not the right thing to be doing.

While not an explicitly articulated experience, several practitioners seemed to feel compelled to enter into a dual or multiple role relationship with a particular client. On occasions, the compulsion appeared to increase the degree of stress encountered by the therapist.

Practitioner harm in a dual or multiple role relationship was usually associated with the impact of stress encountered in complex relationship situations. This was common for those who worked in multi-role jobs where they met clients in a range of roles and contexts. A capacity to recognize and acknowledge the stresses of a dual relationship seemed to actually lessen the stress. One practitioner spoke of the advantages of developing her capacity to tolerate awkwardness and deal with dissonance. As a way of protecting herself from any relational damage, another contributor spoke of developing the capacity to be aware of her own 'stuff' and separate out 'what belonged where'. An individual's stressful reactions could adversely affect their capacity to deal with the situation.

The challenge and conflict of dealing with the various roles was complex and tricky, sometimes compounded by lack of peer or supervisory support. Where these relationships occurred in isolation, without the knowledge or support of others, it appeared more difficult to deal with the challenges that arose. The fact that *some* practitioners found their dual relationship harmful or stressful is significant and carries implications for practitioner training and supervision. Wherever there is potential or actual harm, there are allied ethical and moral questions and basic considerations of right or wrong actions in a given relationship situation. Identifying individuals prone to harm, or the type of dual relationship that is more likely to fail would be useful. Perhaps this signifies positive progress in our attitudes towards duality and complexity in our personal and professional relationships.

THE CHALLENGES OF DUAL RELATIONSHIPS IN TRAINING SETTINGS

Anna's narrative offers helpful insights into several dimensions of being in a dual relationship that arose in a training context. An experienced therapist, trainer and supervisor, Anna spoke of challenges and conflicts where, in the past, she had been therapist, trainer and supervisor to one individual. Although not always a daunting or bad experience, there had been plenty of times of stress and conflict. The therapy and supervisory relationships would tend to extend over a training programme, although some extended beyond the ending of the training period. Early in her career, she did not see overlapping relationships as problematic, but gradually over time and growing knowledge and experience, she felt that they were too problematic and decided to attempt to avoid further dual relationship situations. She found that the dual relationship could prevent the client from discussing or disclosing certain issues and could encourage them to withhold their 'venomous sides or their most crazy sides' for fear of how it might impact on her assessment of them in her training role. Anna spoke at length about her thoughts on the advantages and disadvantages of dual roles in a training context. Her views on the subject echo several other therapist stories, so it is helpful to quote them at length:

> you could do some good cognitive-behavioural therapy, particularly short-term therapy and it wouldn't matter at all if you had another relationship with the person. Perhaps not at the same time, but afterwards . . . plenty of people don't need to do deep work with their early object-relations . . . however, we don't know necessarily if we are taking somebody into long-term therapy, or if it's open-ended therapy. We don't know which of them are going to need to spend some time looking at their very earliest object-relations and therefore we need to . . . make sure that everybody has a safe container which would allow them to do so . . . or, we'll say, yes I do dual relationships, in which case we must be very careful to make it clear that we don't do this sort of therapy, we don't do anything that looks at early developmental stuff . . . but it is very interesting about how passionate we've become about the sanctity of [the therapy] place.

And:

> I know a Jungian analyst [who] says two things; if clients are adults they should be able to behave like robust adults and it's actually not good for them to be protected against reality, that is, to think their therapist hasn't got any other life but them, it encourages them not to cope, function in the world, and I actually agree with that; the other thing he said is that the function of, the aim of analysis, is to get people into being able to have real here-and-now relationships with people instead of those based on complexes and transferences and so on and therefore if he has done successful analysis with someone he would expect to be able to meet them socially because that

person would be able to meet them as their own person; I thought that was a very interesting idea.

Although she thought her colleague's ideas were useful, she also felt that the 'therapy container' (that is what she saw as the potential of the therapy relationship and space to provide a potent arena in which the client can do their work and the therapist can support them in doing the work that they need to do) becomes diluted by a dual relationship:

> gone forever is the possibility of the consulting room being a safe place with boundaries to it . . . a client really needs to feel that they're in a safe relationship, at a safe time, in a safe room in order to get out all the things that are going on inside them and then put them back at the end of the session and go out . . . if you've got an individual in individual therapy they've had to see you with other people [in the training context] long before they planned to do so, so it mucks up the progress of the relationship . . . you are in an assessment role, as supervisor and a trainer I have the power to say 'you're not good enough, you must leave the course' or whatever . . . I'm assessing them rather than being with them, it's a completely, completely different role.

She realized how difficult it was for her to manage the relationship boundaries:

> if I see someone in therapy and I'm also a trainer . . . and a supervisor and responsible for them going through their course and passing their exam and responsible for their clients in a sort of way [through the supervision and training] it is a huge responsibility . . . [when they are the client] they needed to become . . . horrendously dependent . . . and then difficult . . . and so forth . . . if that demand is in carefully prescribed 50 minute chunks then I am available to give myself to it, whereas if I'm also going to be seeing that person next weekend on a training course or next week for supervision . . . and I meet them in the corridor and they say hello to me in that meaning-ful way that makes me think that 'of course, this is X, I need to remember that she needs a particular smile from me'.

Over time and through growing experience and knowledge, this practitioner reached a point where she knew that, for her, some relational places associated with dual relationships were now out of bounds. Anna became aware that some of her dual relationship concerns were less about her inadequacy as a practitioner and more about the roles not being a good mix. She realized that her decision to avoid any further dual relationships was also about her choosing to look after herself and her non-therapy space and contexts. Her values and beliefs had changed over her years of practice and she now felt she could discern whether a particular relational mix might work. The one remaining area where she allowed dual relationships to continue related to relationships formed years ago, where she now had collegial contact – these seemed acceptable to herself and her dual relationship partners.

BEST PRACTICE IN DUAL AND MULTIPLE ROLE RELATIONSHIPS

Practitioners used a range of helpful strategies to support themselves in managing and monitoring the dual relationships, covering several core areas including: contracting; assessing; monitoring, managing and reviewing; and self-development, self-awareness and personal virtues. A well-developed capacity for role fluency was evident in a few of the cases. The strategies shown in the following list were evident across the therapist cases.

Practitioner strategies for monitoring and managing dual and multiple role relationships

Contracting
The processes included:
- agreeing upon role clarity, boundaries and limits of confidentiality.

Assessing
The processes included:
- assessing client capacity to sustain a dual relationship;
- weighing the costs and benefits of a dual relationship;

- using theory to support thinking: for example, psychodynamic, role theory, attachment theory, NLP (neurolinguistic programming).

Monitoring, managing, and reviewing
actions the practitioners took included:
- encouraging mutuality and sharing decision making;
- reviewing unavoidable overlap in a small-town context;
- regularly reviewing the situation;
- reviewing practice and motives for the dual relationship;
- being appropriate with being personal;
- restating the message that it's not friendship but therapy;
- using codes and theories as consultative resources;
- using a peer group for consultative support;
- using supervision to discuss issues related to dual and multiple role relationships;
- doing things related to therapy with the client's full knowledge;
- aiming to be a good rather than a malevolent influence;
- in an organizational context, having clear policies on duality;
- keeping the roles 'context appropriate', that is, when meeting clients outside, they will already have contracted in the therapy relationship for how they want to be greeted (or not);
- 'bracketing' off any prejudice to facilitate being more fully present with the client in the therapy relationship and the overlapping dual or multiple roles.

Self-development, self-awareness, personal virtues and qualities;
the practitioner appeared to:
- have a commitment to personal development through personal therapy, training, supervision, peer group;
- have the capacity for questioning their motives: e.g. why doing this/not doing this?;
- know that on a personal level it might be important and they might want the relationship, but on a professional level, were able to ask 'is it appropriate?' and be able to say 'no' to requests for extra contact;
- equate complying with professional codes with being able to look at self and measure self against the professional standards;
- be ethically aware and have the courage and self assertion to make difficult decisions about the relationship;

- be able to live with the consequences of any decisions and actions;
- develop critical reflexivity.

The most successful dual relationships were recounted by senior, experienced therapists who seemed able to attend to their own psychological, emotional or spiritual needs, thus they did not rely on their dual relationship partner to meet them. These practitioners appeared to have evolved appropriate ways of dealing with the relationship. In view of some practitioners' experiences, we might realistically ask whether training and supervision adequately prepare them to deal with complex relationship situations. Unmistakably, there are limits to what any training or supervisory event can hope or aim to achieve with regard to the personal and professional development of the trainees. Unquestionably, however, it borders the unethical to leave matters of dealing with dual relationships to chance. Where a therapist is unable to fully use their supervision because, for instance, they are at an early stage in the process of developing their practitioner skills and experience, it follows that they need a skilled supervisor who can support them to deal with complex relational situations. However, this assumes that the therapist is willing and able to bring these matters to supervision. It is possible that a practitioner might not trust their supervisor to be able to appropriately support them.

Although some practitioners experienced angst about being in a dual or multiple role relationship, paradoxically, away from a therapy context each of us probably adequately fulfils multiple and diverse roles such as friend, colleague, lover, wife, husband, life partner, parent, sibling or child. Nonetheless, despite our apparent human capacity for role fluency in a range of social and familial contexts, theoretical and pragmatic understanding of complex dual and multiple role relationships is limited. We move on now to look at further ways of considering being in complex relationships.

Chapter 10

Developing a relational ethic for complex relationships

The preceding chapters show clearly that dual and multiple role-relating is complex and challenging. As previously noted, non-therapy, non-sexual contact between clients and their therapists is probably inevitable in some social or cultural contexts (including rural and minority communities) and as such it is important to identify ethically minded and appropriate ways of being in and responding to client–therapist dual and multiple relationships. It is important to remember that what we are talking about here is the need to identify appropriate ways of being in *non-sexual, non-abusive* relationships. The client and practitioner stories point towards a number of key areas associated with dual relationship that we could usefully consider here, with the aim of reaching further understanding and developing resources. These areas consist of: consent to participate; power dynamics; relational capacity; relational responsibility; intentionality; risk assessment; and developing a relational ethic for being in complex relationships.

CONSENT TO PARTICIPATE

Within the helping professions, the client–therapist relationship is widely regarded as a fiduciary relationship founded on a relational bond of implied trust. Merely extending an invitation does not equal client assent, although a therapist might assume so. As the clients' experiences suggest, for them to have an opportunity to comment on their experiences or impressions of the therapist and the dual relationship situation, a genuine invitation that might extend over several occasions must be made, in order to facilitate them in voicing their thoughts and reactions. Consent is best seen as a process rather than a one-off signifying or form-filling event (Grafanaki, 1996; West, 2002). By not inviting or encouraging a client to freely consent to be in the relationship are we abusing their trust in our capacity to make right choices in the relationship?

If we consider Rennie's (1994a) work on client deference, along with the evidence from this study, then difficult questions about client consent become paramount. The following list shows some sample questions, but readers will be able to generate their own.

Examples of questions about client consent

- How can the client freely and truly consent to another role that parallels their current therapy relationship? What processes will help?
- What if . . . the practitioner assumes assent without determining the client's understanding of the relationship?
- What if . . . the practitioner interprets client uncertainty about a dual relationship as negative transference and does not acknowledge a 'real' dimension to their concerns about the relationship?

As noted in Chapter 2, Rennie (1994a) found that clients sometimes defer to the therapist and withhold information about their experiences and perceptions of the relationship. This is significant, especially in relation to establishing whether the client is freely and truly consenting, or whether they are deferring to the more powerful therapist position. A therapist cannot second-guess the client's thoughts and responses to the relationship or its unfolding dynamics, but their theoretical, cultural and personal preferences can inform how they actively seek consent from clients. Therapists from a humanistic approach, such as transactional analysis, are more likely to adopt a loosely held yet robust approach to securing consent, while at the same time seek to involve the client in negotiating the relational conditions. Because of the client–therapist transference relationship, some analytically oriented therapists might balk at the prospect of mutually negotiating a dual relationship with a patient, choosing not to enter into a dual relationship. However, our social and cultural communities are becoming increasingly complex and diverse and it is likely that our clients will at some point, in some way, overlap from the therapy setting in which we meet with them, into other social or professional arenas. While a client might give their consent to overlapping contact, at the same time, they might feel unable to challenge the situation. This is borne out by several client-contributors in this study whose deference or acquiescence helped them avoid a rejection from their therapist, loss of the therapist, or loss of a perceived safe space. Clearly, then, clients, and therapists can be confused and ambivalent in dual relationship situations. Unquestionably, however, there are major moral and ethical implications if the client's understanding of the relational situation and interactions is not considered (Pope and Vasquez, 1998).

In relation to cultural dimensions of a dual relationship, a white middle-class Western European practitioner working with clients from other cultures needs to identify and explore their beliefs and practices in order to recognize and pre-empt discriminatory or disrespectful practices. Increasingly, we encounter situations of diverse or conflicting cultural views on what are appropriate ways of being and relating in one-to-one or community relationships (see, for example, Sue and Sue, 2003; Syme, 2003). In the role of practitioner, we can seek ways to explore the relational situation that do not diminish the integrity and validity of either individual's cultural preferences and ways of assenting. Of course, we can never fully anticipate future events or situations, but we can rehearse them in our mind, or with our dual relationship partners or in supervisory contexts.

In this study, as shown in Chapter 8, some clients attempted to influence the relationship by remaining silent, or by revealing only part of their response to the situation. Rennie's (2000) finding, that in the reflexive moment the client can choose between thinking and saying what they are thinking, is significant here. While his research is not about dual relationships, importantly, it explores the client's experience of being in a helping relationship.

> The client's assumption of control by choosing to think without expressing the thinking imposes a constraint on what the therapist can know about what the client is feeling and doing in any given moment. At the same time, this does not mean that clients may not necessarily reveal to the therapist what they are experiencing if asked. When their thinking has to do with clients' following their own leads, they may welcome an invitation to say what they are thinking . . . [Y]et, when the client is inwardly dealing with a disjunction of some sort, and especially a disjunction having to do with the therapist, a

probe into it may be experienced as a threat to the control to which they are adhering, and especially when the client is interested in preserving the relationship with the therapist. In this circumstance, although they may still resist risking disclosure, it may be easier for clients to respond to the therapist opening up a dialogue about the disjunction than it is for them to do so themselves.

(Rennie, 2000: 164)

Given that a client's response might not only be transferential but might also relate to the 'real' relationship between the client and therapist (Greenson, 1967; Rennie, 2000), the therapist in a dual relationship situation needs to be especially alert to the client's communication in the relationship and create opportunities for metacommunication, whereby the individuals reflect on and evaluate the relationship, informing its progress.

POWER DYNAMICS

Arguably, an important aspect in the prevention of harm, as several of the clients' experiences show, is acknowledgment of power dynamics in the client–practitioner and overlapping dual or multiple roles. For example, the client whose words are shown at the beginning of Chapter 8 felt trapped and had great difficulty extracting herself from a destructive multiple role relationship. Unable to tell anyone about her predicament, she was alone and vulnerable. Recognition that there is potential for abusive use of power in the helping relationship has led to tightly defined codes of ethics (McLeod, 1998). In a non-sexual dual or multiple role relationship there are probably complex links between power, autonomy and trust. For instance, by virtue of the therapist's professional role and associated power and authority, some client-participants invested them with a more powerful status and identity in the relationship, thus minimizing their own power.

Pope, Levenson and Schover (1979) surveyed women students and found that 72 per cent who had sexual contact with their tutors felt no coercion at the time of the contact, but by the time of the survey this had shifted to only 49 per cent believing no coercion took place. Although these findings relate to student–tutor sexual dual relationships, they correlate with Russell's (1993) research with counselling and psychotherapy clients, which showed that many clients' interpretations and perceptions of relationship events changed over time. According to Russell, this might be due to the client's ambivalent responses at the time, as well as the result of a lack of clear contracting. With clients' perceptions and interpretations changing over time, this will have major implications for the therapist's method of managing a dual relationship. As Russell points out, a client's confusion might increase when the therapist lacks the basic communication skills to clarify the situation with the client (Russell, 1993). If, as Russell suggests, many clients have overt or covert experience of a previous abusive relationship, then checking out the client's understanding of the relational processes is paramount. Arguably, awareness of the intention of our interventions is not enough if we then fail to check out the client's understanding of our action. However, an intentionally abusive therapist is not likely to want to ascertain whether the client understands the nature of the abuse.

According to studies of therapist characteristics and their impact on the client, persuasive qualities such as perceived expertness, attractiveness and trustworthiness can positively influence the process and outcome of the therapy (Beutler *et al.*, 1994). It is feasible, then, to imagine a client's being impressed or seduced by their perceptions of the therapist's qualities and 'agreeing' to enter into overlapping dual or multiple roles. Equally, as the client-contributors' experiences testify, it is possible for a client to place themselves or feel pressured into a position of having less power in the relationship and consequently feel coerced into non-therapy contact (Pearson and Piazza, 1997). This scenario becomes especially problematic where the therapist is intentionally or unintentionally abusive. A 'predatory professional' (Pearson and Piazza, 1997) will intentionally abuse their more powerful professional position in the therapy relationship in order to influence the client to perform certain tasks or enter into roles. Alarmingly, the client might naïvely trust that the therapist, in their abusive actions, is 'caring' for them (Russell, 1993). This is not so surprising if we consider that a proportion of clients will have been abused in childhood and therefore might be unable to protect themselves from further abuse.

BPS (1997) has cautioned that power imbalances exist in dual relationship situations, although it advises against assuming that these relationships are exploitative or always lead to negative consequences. At the same time, it acknowledged a need for psychological models that possess 'explanatory power' in dual relationships (BPS, 1997: 36). However, identifying explanatory models is not easy. The complexities of the helping situation – for instance, the setting or cultural context in which it occurs, the therapist and their characteristics, the client and their characteristics, the therapeutic orientation, and the duration and type of therapy – constitute a dynamic interplay of contributing features. In a review of research on client variables and therapy outcomes, Garfield (1994: 220) concluded variables and findings can be so diverse that 'it would appear worthwhile for each clinical setting to evaluate its own pattern of continuation and outcome'. An appraisal of relational power in dual relationships needs the kind of local or situated approach advocated by Garfield. Clients are as diverse as practitioners and some can and will take more responsibility for sharing relational power earlier on, while others might need responsible and careful holding. These lines of thought generate similar questions to those raised in the earlier section on relationship responsibility.

Examples of questions related to power dynamics in the relationship
- Who is responsible for assessing relational features and managing the progress of the power dynamics? The therapist? The client? Both?
- How can issues or concerns about relational power be mutually processed in a relationship or role in which the parties are unequal?
- Should the practitioner have the key role in supporting and shaping the dual relationship?
- How can the practitioner best support and encourage the client to assess their own needs and preferences in the relationship?

Relational power in a dual relationship is probably best viewed as a dynamic interpersonal construct rather than a static entity. This line of thinking is consistent with feminist and social constructionist readings of power in relational situations (Chaplin, 1988; McNamee and Gergen, 1992, 1999; Noddings, 2002; Proctor, 2002; Russell, 1993). We might construe power as an interconnection and interaction of relational forces that compete and accede in a constant dynamic interplay. Ideally, both parties would have an awareness and understanding of the 'power-plays' in the relationship, as they occur. Realistically, however, some clients and therapists will be inexperienced and lack the skills to enable them to do this. Moreover, in a relationship where a therapist is intentionally abusive, relational mutuality will not exist. A practitioner's theoretical preferences will also dictate to what degree mutuality is sought.

RELATIONAL CAPACITY

Being robust enough to deal with relational ambiguity, conflict and stress is probably a significant factor in 'surviving' the complexities of being in a dual or multiple role relationship. The client and practitioner stories bear witness to this. Ideally, a practitioner's core training and postgraduate practicum period would encompass developing an understanding and experience of managing complex relational dynamics, including dual relationships. Essentially, this develops our capacity for role fluency (Clarkson, 1994: 2000). While role fluency is useful for both practitioner and client, the client might not be able to deal with multiple or complex roles and in some cases a dual relationship might be inadvisable for them. Equally, cultural differences might generate context-specific challenges. For example, Syme (2003) raises questions about working with clients whose basic needs are for pragmatic support with, for example, form-filling. Syme also notes that in the case of Maori and Samoan people, when an issue is particularly sensitive, such as sexual abuse, one person is given spokesperson's right for the family (Syme, 2003: 121). Transcultural and interpersonal relating is complex and demands sensitive and respectful relational dynamics.

We probably assume too much about clients' and therapists' capacity to be in diverse or conflicting relationship settings and forget that most therapists are or will have been clients themselves. Myths of the 'therapized' or 'sussed therapist' are not rare and might link with fear of others seeing us as a wounded healer or flawed therapist, suggesting we need to question our assumptions and perceptions of competency. Professional bodies are increasingly focusing on practitioners' capacity to maintain their competence and care for self. For example, BACP (2002) affords self-care equal status with key moral principles for helping practice. We can legitimately question a therapist's capacity for dealing with complex relational situations, but we cannot presume that all therapists who enter into dual relationships lack integrity. A key context in which practitioners develop their competency is training and ability to be in helping relationships. The person-centred approach places our capacity to form intimate and restorative relationships at its core. As discussed in Chapter 2, Mearns uses the notion of over- or under-involvement as one way of noting how we engage with and experience being in relationship with the client. However, developing a sensitive and responsive relational ethic for dealing with complex relationships such as dual relationships is unlikely to feature prominently in practitioner-training programmes.

The power of a secure base, represented in the practitioner and the relationship, to represent and provide safety suggests there is scope for great confusion if this perceived base then becomes unsafe. In attachment terms, a 'perverse paradox' develops when the caregiver (in this case, the practitioner) is both a key attachment figure to whom the client turns and the source of threat (Holmes, 2001: 96). Where the client is in an abusive or harmful dual relationship and the practitioner is a key caregiver, they might be ambivalent about whether the relationship is safe.

While we might assume that an experienced therapist in the role of 'client' could be self-supporting in a dual relationship, the client and practitioner experiences suggest otherwise. We cannot ignore the fact that all clients and practitioners were themselves therapists at the time of contributing their story. In addition, many clients were either trained or trainee therapists at the time of the dual relationship. Even cases where the client was an experienced therapist at the time of the dual relationship did not offer 'protection' to them in their client role. These facts are critical. Significantly, for clients who themselves were trained or trainee therapists, they suggest that the emotional potency and stress generated by the relational situation can override prior knowledge and understanding of therapy processes. This suggests that we need to be especially vigilant about a client's capacity to care for self in a dual relationship situation. Some dual relationship partners seemed a better 'fit' than others, with successful cases typified by either a client who was able to sustain themselves in a relationship or a client who was partnered with a current or former therapist who appeared to be supportive and non-abusive. There seems to be a case here for being sufficiently psychologically robust before entering into a dual relationship.

RELATIONAL RESPONSIBILITY

Few would disagree that therapists carry a moral responsibility for and duty of care towards their clients, involving obligations not to cause harm. More contentious perhaps are matters related to the demand this professional obligation places on the therapist and the associated need for a certain degree of personal and professional resourcefulness and robustness (Baker, 2003). We might question where, how and in what roles relational responsibility operates. In this study, therapist-participants who successfully managed dual and multiple role relationships communicated an image of a competent and compassionate dual relationship partner who involved the client in deciding relational matters across the various roles they shared. In most cases, the therapist communicated an attitude of being open to learning and willing to see the dual relationship partner as an equal in the co-construction of the relationship. Conversely, there was striking evidence in several of the client stories to suggest that their therapist was not a caring dual relationship partner and did not exercise a duty of care in any of the relationship roles. Quite the opposite seemed to occur and in several cases clients were debilitated by the experience.

Perceptions of relational responsibility are likely to shift according to beliefs, skills and practices as well as the influences of culture, society and professional context. A person-centred therapist might see it as the client's responsibility to raise any relational concern they have. On the other hand, a psychodynamic therapist might interpret the client's reactions to the relationship as transference dynamics rather than any manifestation of a real relationship between client and therapist. The client cases suggested few of their practitioners attended to the ethics of the relationship. The profession and the public expect that therapists will be responsible and provide a good standard of care for their clients, yet a significant feature of many client stories was that the therapist did not appear to care.

In the case of a dual relationship where a current therapy relationship is overlapped by a business relationship, then it is the therapist's responsibility to intervene and check out their partner's understanding of the relational situation as well as their reactions to it. Arguably, seeking to identify the client's understanding and awareness of the relational processes and events constitutes a professional obligation on the therapist's part, which thus becomes part of the therapist's intent in the relationship. A practitioner might assume their current or former client can take responsibility for their decisions and actions in the dual relationship, when in fact they cannot, or do not know how to, do this for themselves. For example, if a client fears losing their therapist, they might withhold their feelings and responses in order to avoid any rejection and ultimately, avoid any loss. A fear of loss of relationship was evident in several client stories, apparently influencing whether and how they withheld their responses and feelings from their dual relationship partner.

Both Lewin's (1948) notion of field theory and Norsworthy and Gerstein's (2003) ideas on how to develop collaborative and facilitative relationships in states or events that are in constant flux offer useful resources. In addition, the growing literature on systemic, social constructionist, narrative, feminist, multicultural, peace and conflict resolution theories provide excellent materials through which to develop our own thinking and understanding of being in complex relationship situations. For further useful resources, see Sue and Sue (2003) in relation to multicultural theory and practice. Additionally, Brown (1994), Heyward (1993), Noddings (2002) and Sherwin (2001) offer excellent resources for feminist thinking on mutual and collaborative relationships, while Winslade and Monk (2000) provide useful resources on narrative approaches to conflict resolution.

Codes of ethics and frameworks for ethical practice rightly identify the therapist's responsibility for the therapy relationship and work, yet do not consider any client responsibility. In the successful client and practitioner dual relationships in this study both partners actively and consciously collaborated to manage the relationship. This included taking decisions on transitions from one role or type of relationship to another. In other cases, usually the unsuccessful or harmful ones, relational matters seemed a matter of chance, suggesting that the therapist made assumptions about, or ignored, the client's capacity to sustain the relationship. In cases of successful dual relationships, therapist-participants appeared able to draw on their personal, professional and theoretical knowledge and skills to inform their relational decisions and actions.

From the discussions so far, we can generate a range of questions about relational responsibility and dual relationships.

Examples of questions about relational responsibility

- At what point post-therapy do we decide that it is appropriate to shift responsibilities and enter into a dual relationship?
- How long, say, after the formation of a post-therapy friendship relationship does the former therapist have to afford a duty of care to the former client?
- Is it a case of once a client always a client?
- What place, if any, does the notion of client responsibility hold in this situation?
- What are the responsibilities of each individual, in each role?
- Does the practitioner's duty of care extend to all of the dual or multiple roles?
- Whose responsibility is it to monitor the compassion and care for the individual who was formerly the client?

INTENTIONALITY

The idea of therapist intentionality is beginning to appear in therapy-related literature (see, for example, Gabriel and Davies, 2000; Russell, 1993, 1999). It can refer to intent associated with choice of therapeutic intervention (Russell, 1999) and I use it here in a similar way to convey the intentions and subsequent actions of persons-in-relationship. At first glance, the notion of intentionality might seem to be more the therapist's domain and responsibility, yet the client's intentions will also be significant in the process and outcome of the dual relationship. Clients' responsibilities and obligations in the relationship are likely to be of a different kind or order from those of the practitioner. The greater our awareness of how we make decisions about our actions, the better the prospects for the relationship. An individual's intent within a dual relationship is likely to correspond with the role they are enacting and its assumed or expressed responsibilities. However, intent can become confused where individuals are unsure of themselves in the relationship. For example, one client-participant was in a multiple role relationship with her therapist and found it difficult to know how to be in each of the different relationships she held with her. These included business, social and therapy relationships. Perhaps it is hardly surprising that she was ambiguous about the relationship roles. If her dual relationship partner had supported a process of mutual clarification, the outcome might not have been so destructive or damaging.

Ideally, dual relationship partners would mutually identify and agree their relationship obligations. As therapists, we need to initiate and facilitate this process, relinquishing this more powerful position as the client develops their capacity to contribute to mutually influence the course and direction of the relationship. How simple this process sounds in a narrative form, yet the words belie the complexity of the lived experience. Without a doubt, trusting the integrity of one's intent will challenge our self-awareness and understanding of being in relationship with self and others.

RISK ASSESSMENT

While the idea of risk assessment of the client (Heard and Lake, 1997), the therapist (Holmes, 2000) or the dual relationship (Pearson and Piazza, 1997) might be novel, it is not inappropriate or impossible. Practitioner training might not adequately address assessment (Reeves, Wheeler and Bowl, 2004) yet forms of client assessment already exist in the helping field. For instance, the *DSM-IV-TR* (American Psychiatric Association, 2000) is used in NHS contexts to assess and diagnose psychological states such as symbiotic or borderline psychoses. This process assumes, of course, a particular theoretical and clinical stance and not all therapies or therapists will advocate assessment informed by a medical model of review and diagnoses.

Some theoretical approaches and practitioners might disagree with any form of client assessment. For example, from a person-centred position, Mearns has argued that client assessment runs counter to person-centred theory, is more apt in approaches that adopt a medical model style of working and no research satisfactorily demonstrates the validity or reliability of client assessment procedures (Mearns, 1997). A psychodynamic or analytical practitioner is more likely to address issues of patient/client assessment, whereas a person-centred counsellor might view this as compromising relational spontaneity and immediacy, as well as objectifying the client (Ruddle, 1997). Importantly, Mearns's objections were raised in the specific context of assessing clients for allocation to suitable counsellors in an agency setting, whereas the process of assessment imagined here is more about client protection and therapist pre-paredness in a potentially tricky dual relationship situation.

Some humanistic practitioners do acknowledge that pragmatic assessment can be helpful in deciding whether a client is appropriate for counselling and can sufficiently contain themselves to carry on in their work and life (Rowan, 1998). A practitioner might work with an individual whose sense of self and boundaries of the self in relation to 'where I begin and end and where you begin and end' are fragile or distorted. In this type of case, there is an ethical imperative to assess the client's capacity to sustain the relationship. Where a client is diagnosed as psychotic, they are likely to be viewed as incapable of separating out psychologically from the therapy or the therapist and thus would be unable to sustain themselves through diverse and multiple roles with the therapist. Work with individuals diagnosed as having borderline personality disorder suggests that the more psychologically disorganized or distressed the individual, the greater the need for an objective third-party stance through which to review the situation (Hedges, 1997). However, such diagnostic 'labelling' of a client's psychological state has been criticised for its objectification of the individual and the omission of the client's subjective experience (Rowan, 1998).

Assessment could identify skills or qualities that are likely to help or hinder the relationship. For example, an individual with a history of violent childhood sexual abuse is likely to need clearly defined, compassionate boundary-holding, suggesting that a complex dual relationship, involving multiple roles, will probably be problematic. Additional support, in the guise of peer and/or supervisor review, could be a valuable part of holding and monitoring the processes and progress of the dual relationship and its various roles. Resources to support bespoke assessment and ethical decision-making are becoming increasingly available (see, for example, Clarkson, 2000; Gabriel and Casemore, 2003; Jones et al., 2000; Palmer Barnes and Murdin, 2001). Both the clients' and the practitioners' experiences shown earlier generate questions about an individual's emotional and psychological 'readiness' or 'robustness' for being in a dual or multiple role relationship. Perhaps the ideal situation is one where the capacity to sustain self in a dual relationship can be identified and evaluated in some way. Exactly how this might work in practice is unknown. However, knowledge of relational style might be one useful way to predict the possible progression or outcome of the dual relationship (Gabriel, 2001c).

The Adult Attachment Interview (AAI) (Main, Kaplan and Cassidy, 1985) uses a semi-structured interview to assess the interviewee's attachment style. Combined with Mallinckrodt and colleagues' Client Attachment to Therapist Scale (Mallinckrodt, Coble and Gantt, 1995; Mallinckrodt, Gantt and Coble, 1995), it is possible that adapted versions could provide tools for assessing attachment style and predicting those clients or therapists for whom a dual relationship is contra-indicated. An AAI-informed assessment might identify an individual's capacity for 'narrative competence' and 'reflexive self function' (Holmes, 1996: 12). Reflexive self-function refers to the capacity to think about self in relation to others. This ability is thought to be important protection against psychological vulnerability in the face of environmental threat or difficulty (Holmes, 1996). In a dual or multiple role relationship, then, one's ability to reflect on and understand the relational dynamics might be a reasonable indicator of one's capacity to sustain self in the relationship. Narrative competence is an indicator of psychological capacity. In attachment theory the idea of achieving a cohesive narrative thread that runs through the client's perceptions of self, other and life in general forms a significant part of the work (Fish and Dudas, 1999; McLeod 1999b).

Attachment theory acknowledges the significance of intimacy, loss and separation issues in human relationships – relational experiences that might be encountered within in the context of a dual relationship. Part of attachment theory's power and appeal rest in its non-pathological approach to human relationships. Contrary to most psychodynamic approaches, it emphasizes security in human relationships rather than sexuality (Holmes, 1997a). With its roots in traditional psychoanalytic approaches, it has shoots in contemporary social psychology. According to Bowlby, attachment behaviour comprises the actions and interactions that enable a person to attain or retain proximity to some other differentiated and preferred individual, usually conceived as stronger and/or wiser (Bowlby, 1979). Bowlby believed that this proximity-seeking behaviour establishes a secure base from which to embark on exploration into the unknown. An individual tends towards secure or insecure attachments to significant others. In the context of the therapy relationship, Bowlby saw it as the therapist's role to provide a secure base in order to facilitate the client's psychological explorations and the challenging of their working models (their inner representations of self and relationships with others) (Bowlby, 1979). In the relationship, then, the client forms an attachment to the therapist, based on their internal working models that are representational of early, formative attachments with primary caregivers.

Attachment bonds are thought to be relatively long-enduring (Gross, 1997) with an individual tending towards either secure or insecure attachments. The aim of an individual's attachment behaviour, or as I see it, attachment style, is to provide a secure base (Bowlby, 1969) both in reality and as an internal representation (Holmes, 1997b) from which to explore the environment (Bowlby, 1969). According to attachment theory, then, we seek closeness (physical or symbolic) to our attachment figures such as our parents or caregivers (Bowlby, 1969) and can experience separation anxiety when distanced from them (Gross, 1997). Bowlby saw secure or insecure attachment as a core determinant of an individual's behaviour in relationships (Holmes, 1993). Secure attachment is thought to promote the development of self-worth and maturity and enhance the development of autonomy and the capacity for intimacy in relationships (Holmes, 1993). Thus, a securely attached individual will possess the capacity to mediate a range of relationship roles (Holmes, 1993). Mallinckrodt and his colleagues (Mallinckrodt, Coble and Gantt, 1995; Mallinckrodt, Gantt and Coble, 1995) found those with a secure attachment style are more likely to form positive transferences to their therapist. Equally, those with fearful or avoidant attachment patterns are more likely to form negative transference attachments to the therapist.

Hazan and Shaver (1987) usefully outline three adult attachment typologies that might form part of a dual relationship assessment tool:

1   **Secure:** I find it relatively easy to get close to others and am comfortable depending on them and having them depend on me. I don't worry about being abandoned or about someone getting too close to me.
2   **Insecure avoidant:** I am somewhat uncomfortable being close to others; I find it difficult to trust them completely, difficult to allow myself to depend on them. I am nervous when anyone gets too close, and often, partners want me to be more intimate than I feel comfortable being.

3   **Insecure anxious/ambivalent:** I find that others are reluctant to get as close as I would like. I often worry that my partner doesn't really love me or won't want to stay with me. I want to merge completely with another person and this desire sometimes scares people away.

A client might regard their therapist as a significant attachment figure (Pistole, 1989). Without doubt, the therapeutic relationship and the therapist's role as an attachment figure will take on additional and challenging relational dimensions where dual or multiple role relationships are involved. Certainly, as a conceptual tool for gaining insight into affectional bonds, attachment theory has made a significant contribution in the fields of psychology and psychotherapy (Heard and Lake, 1997; Holmes, 1996, 2000). In the context of dual relationships, it might provide a way to think about the capacity of the individuals involved to cope with being in the relationship, as well as gain some understanding of the dynamics that occur. Applying attachment theory to managing relational proximity or distance, or attachment and loss issues in the context of a dual relationship might throw light on how to assess for and deal with the relational situation. Where a client shows an anxious, avoidant or disorganized attachment, then a dual relationship is contra-indicated. Individuals with insecure attachments might need long-term supportive therapy and a dual relationship is therefore inadvisable. The more insecure an individual's attachment style, the less likely they will be able to cope with the complexities of dual or multiple role-relating.

The idea of assessing a *therapist's* capacity for a particular dual relationship does not feature in the literature. Yet an important part of offering self as a helper is a capacity and willingness to reflect upon our personal morals, qualities, strengths and limitations, as well as how we relate in relationships. If not, then as therapist, how can we be sure about what impact we have on the client and the therapy work? Importantly, in a complex dual role situation, how can we be clear about how we are influencing the client, the relationship and various relationship roles? Research suggests that an insecurely attached client in a therapy relationship with an insecurely attached therapist will elicit increasingly more care from the therapist (Holmes, 2000). Conversely, securely attached therapists are likely to be firm with their boundaries (Holmes, 2000).

DEVELOPING A RELATIONAL ETHIC FOR COMPLEX RELATIONSHIPS

While it might be comforting to be able to refer to a quick guide to dealing with particular dual and multiple role relationships, the individual nature of each relational experience does not allow for this. Obviously, we can refer to ethical and relational 'benchmarks', such as BACP's Ethical Framework (2002), but ultimately they remain guidelines and cannot account for the nuances of the unique relational situation. That is the task of the therapist and their dual relationship partner. Undoubtedly, as the client and practitioner experiences in this study suggest, this is a challenging and conflicted process, as well as potentially damaging.

When circumstantial or intentional dual and multiple role-relating occurs, how can we militate against damage and harm? Ideally, dual relationship partners would negotiate and share the responsibility, moving away from perceiving relational responsibility as a task or function that resides exclusively with one or other party (usually the person in the position of 'expert' or the figure of authority). While the role of therapist attracts particular notions of responsibility and obligation, it should not assume greater status in the relationship. For example, if you consult a medical specialist you do expect her/him to be an expert in their field, although you do not necessarily regard them as a better/more powerful human being. The client–practitioner dual relationship can be viewed as a collaborative effort, with the practitioner obligated to raise relational issues, facilitating the client's capacity for mutual decision-making in the relationship roles and facilitating the development of shared responsibility until the client–dual relationship partner can mobilize their personal and interpersonal responsibility.

The client and practitioner dual relationship experiences in this study occurred in a range of environments and encompassed diverse contextual features. In Chapter 9, Carol's practitioner experience of working with clients across a range of settings and in different role identities, including advocacy and mentoring, is likely to echo the situations of increasing numbers of practitioners working in multi-role or multi-task jobs. Practitioners are increasingly required to work in diverse cultural, social and organizational settings and therefore need to be aware of a wide range of cultural bases in order to effectively and respectfully work inter- and cross-culturally (Sue and Sue, 2003). Within the clients' experiences shown in Chapter 5, Rachel's account of working as a colleague with her current therapist illustrates the kinds of challenges that can arise for the dual relationship that combines the therapy work and relationship with organizational culture and context.

In keeping with McNamee and Gergen's (1999) approach to relational obligations, the relationship can involve conjoint responsibility – a situation where the parties share responsibility for the relationship's progress. This resonates with Spinelli's (2001, 2003) idea that choice and responsibility within the therapy relationship are interpersonal dimensions. Individual capacity for this conjoint responsibility will vary. We could envision it as a dialogue between the individuals and particularities of the situation, event or experience.

A focus on personal, interpersonal, cultural and contextual dimensions of relating and meaning-making is evident in social constructionist and interpretive theory and practice. A long-standing Western European focus on individualism is gradually shifting to accommodate postmodern notions of self-in-relation, accommodating a multidimensional view of reality that acknowledges the impact of relationships and context on our experiences and perceptions. Our capacity for moral reasoning is influenced by context, not just self, and, as Parker asserts, needs to be 'a relational, embodied dialogue between human beings struggling to make sense of deeply perplexing situations' (Parker, 1991: 37). Additionally, the status or identity of what constitutes an issue or dilemma in a dual relationship might vary between individuals and contexts. What becomes perceived or defined as a dilemma or ethical matter will differ between different theoretical or philosophical perspectives (MacKay and O'Neill, 1992), yet a feminist practitioner might argue that all relational interactions should be regarded as ethical endeavours (Brown, 1991). Recognition of the interconnected nature of human relationships and the capacity of the practitioner to ethically manage the relational situation features in the work of Beauchamp and Childress (1994). Their 'coherence theory' incorporates a principled ethical and moral framework involving both inductive and deductive reasoning and decision-making alongside a relational focus and a recognition of the particular case or situation.

Practitioners aim for a stance of 'compassionate detachment' (Beauchamp and Childress, 1994: 468; Gabriel, 1999). Through mutual regard and responsibility, this compassionate distance

(Beauchamp and Childress, 1994; Gabriel, 1999) will support the relationship. Arguably, this approach demands a great deal of the human therapist with his or her idiosyncratic preferences, performances, skills and abilities. Importantly, it would involve looking beyond theoretical posturing and personal rhetoric to encompass wider relational issues, including relationship context, to embody a collaborative and multidimensional approach to ethics and relational thinking and practice. A relational ethic is best thought of as a particular way of being in relationship. Unmistakably, personal and professional preferences will uniquely influence and shape the quality, process and progress of each individual practitioner's relational ethic.

A feminist-influenced relational ethic

Feminist ethics stand out as a source of alternative responses for ethical and moral discourse and decision-making (Heyward, 1993; Koehn, 1998; Sherwin, 2001; Tong, Anderson and Santos, 2001). Although not explicitly feminist in orientation, the relational ethic I am suggesting here would draw on feminist-informed approaches to ethical inquiry. At best, feminist approaches offer a focus on the relational, identify the complexity and interconnectedness of relational conditions and attend to the power and gender dynamics inherent in the relationship. According to Gilligan (1982), there are two broad types of moral decision-making; a traditional, male-oriented, rule-bound approach and a female-oriented care ethic. Moving away from a traditional ethics stance exemplified by objectivity and detachment, she focuses on the centrality of narrative and relational details in moral decision-making. Gilligan's approach suggests a way of engaging with ethical and moral matters that values the particular (that is, an individual and local experience), the concrete (that which is embodied, situated and contextual) and the relational (that which pertains to relationship(s)). Such an approach seems relevant to counselling and therapy, where there is a focus on relational matters and of course in a dual relationship, where we need awareness of the impact of dual or multiple roles and the context in which the relationship occurs.

Koehn (1998: 148–56), for example, suggests a dialogical ethic that provides 'principles for disciplined thoughtfulness . . . [and] continuing thoughtfulness . . . [that] would seem to be the source of any rightness the act may possess'. She argues that a discursive ethic of 'ongoing thoughtfulness' is an appropriate way to assess the rightness of decisions and actions. Nevertheless, this is not an undisciplined approach, as she also claims that individuals need to be open to rigorous debate in order to select the best action and avoid doing wrong. In keeping with feminist traditions, she advocates a relational perspective, but also argues for a defensible ethic that stands critical scrutiny.

Both Koehn and Gilligan exemplify an ethical stance that brings with it an acute awareness of the implications and consequences of relationship context. This degree of awareness might be necessary for a successful therapy or dual relationship ethic; a relational condition echoed by Pope's challenging comment on the moral and ethical features of sexual activity between a client and their therapist:

> Counselors [sic] may be aware that they are violating ethical, legal, clinical, and professional standards – and are taking a personal risk – when they engage in sex with their clients. But they tend to be unaware of the devastating ways in which they are violating the client's welfare, trust, sense of identity, and potential for future development.
>
> (Pope, 1988a: 223)

Ideally, in a dual relationship the partners will interact in the roles and form shared understandings. One way of developing this into clinical practice might be through contracting and regular, ongoing, mutual reviews of the relationship processes and progression. Matters of relational fidelity, keeping trust and providing an ethic of care will be central.

Developing a personal relational ethic

A personal relational ethic might involve a range of features including: an assessment of the intent and purpose of the relationship; a willingness and capacity to support the client in navigating uncharted relational territory; a consideration of the context in which the relationship occurs; an assessment of the emotional and psychological needs and capacity of the individuals currently or previously in the role of client and therapist; a recognition of the emotional and psychological capabilities and limits of both the

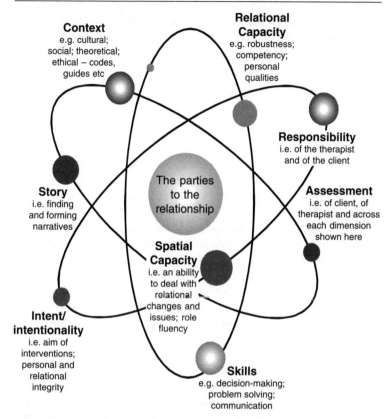

Figure 10.1 A retational ethic.

client and therapist and their capacity to engage in and sustain themselves in a dual relationship and an awareness of the relational responsibilities.

Figure 10.1 shows dimensions that may interact and constellate to form a relational ethic for complex relationships such as a dual relationship. It is shown as an orrery, a model of the planetary system in our galaxy. The model creatively lends itself to a vision of a relational ethic. Arising from ongoing astronomical discoveries, the constellation is constantly shifting, expanding and changing – not unlike human relating, hence the value of this type of model as a framework for developing a relational ethic.

Three assumptions are central to the relational ethic conceived here: (i) static security is illusory; (ii) constant flux is the norm; and,

(iii) paradoxical forces are inherent in relational contexts and situations. The interaction of the different 'spheres' or dimensions of each unique relationship situation will constitute an iterative process, moving back and forth, combining elements of past with the here and now, to form the moving on/future. A capacity to withstand conflict, ambiguity and chaos, as well as develop conciliation and mediation skills to arbitrate between the different dimensions, will form some of the qualities, skills and ways of being involved in making it work. Each dimension will interact differently, according to various internal and external influences. For example, a client or practitioner's personal relationships (*context*), their theoretical or philosophical beliefs (again, *context*), their capacity to be in the relationship and its dual or multiple roles (the *relational* and *spatial* dimensions) and the relationship environment (again, *context*) in which they play out, might adversely (or beneficially) influence the progress of the client–practitioner work and relationship. Essentially, the process involves developing ethical literacy (Gabriel, 2001a), with the person in the role of practitioner (or perhaps previously in the role of practitioner) taking responsibility for generating conversations and reviews or assessments with the client about relational issues (*intentionality, responsibility* and *assessment* dimensions).

As part of this process, and particularly in the early phases of the relationship, the practitioner-dual relationship partner can take up their sentinel role. It is in this role of sentinel that the practitioner is also the boundary rider (Gabriel, 1996; Gabriel and Davies, 2000; Syme, 2003), guarding the integrity of the relationship.

Chapter 11

Concluding comments

Throughout the last few years of being involved in researching dual relationships, I am constantly reminded of how theoretical, professional and cultural context influences our perceptions of these relationships. For example, at the time of my original research into client and practitioner experiences, I encountered a range of negative and hostile responses to my inquiry. In addition, there were individuals who did offer to participate, then withdrew. Responses from non-participants to my request for contributors suggest some individuals were anxious or uncertain about contributing. Several responded to my request for contributions by noting that they would not consider entering into a dual relationship because of their theoretical orientation and professional preferences. The following comments convey the range of responses:

> As a psychodynamic practitioner it would be extremely unlikely for me to be involved in a dual relationship. In principle, I think it is unhelpful and makes work in the transference more complex. I have not done it to date and have no plans to do so.

> From my standpoint (psychoanalytical) there should be *no* such relationships – they would be undesirable sequentially and impossible concurrently if any meaningful work is to be achieved in the therapy.

> I'm fortunate enough to be able to choose who I work with and am therefore able to avoid dual relationship.

> I am puzzled at your research. I do realize that not everyone feels as I do, but I see dangers where boundaries are confused,

not the least being that where a client is also friend/partner/ colleague of her therapist she unconsciously expects the therapy relationship to continue into other areas of life.

I have never counselled anyone with whom I have another role-relationship and I will not consider seeing a therapist with whom I was in another role-relationship either.

I was surprised to receive your request for experiences of dual relationships in counselling. I had thought it was a basic tenet of counselling that you do not ever counsel someone with whom you have (or have had) some other relationship. There are many reasons for this, all of which are outlined in the literature.

My impression from these comments is that dual and multiple role relationships continue to be a taboo area. Implicit in these responses is a care about ethical relating. However, as noted in preceding chapters, our working landscape is changing, diversifying and increasingly being lived out within complex cultural contexts. We cannot ignore the fact that dual and multiple role-relating does exist and will continue to do so. I think it is no accident that several contributors who provided documentary evidence spelt 'dual' as 'duel', indicating the potential for conflict in dual and multiple role-relating. My hope is that this text will help to engender further debate and literature on being in complex relationships, as well as provide accessible resource. We need further discourse in a wide range of contexts, including the professional literature, practitioner training and supervision. Sustained and detailed narratives are probably one of the best mediums through which to convey much-needed accounts and resources on dual relationships. For instance, clients' and practitioners' accounts of their experiences can be regarded as moral stories that convey the role and impact of 'failure' or 'success' in relational choices and actions, as well as the participants' experiences and perceptions of these. Readers of the stories contained in this text, for example, can adapt them in order to make sense of their own situation.

I agree with McLeod's contention (1997: 46) that 'a story can provide a guideline or "script" for how to behave in social situations' and that 'stories move people' (McLeod, 1997: 43). In addition, I also share Etherington's assertion that '[A] story is full and rich, coming as it does out of personal and social history. People lead storied lives and tell stories of those lives' (Etherington, 2000: 298). Critically, the story format can convey a moral tale in a situated way and is thus likely to have more meaning for consumers of the story (for example therapists, clients, training providers, supervisors, supervisory consultants). The impact on generations of children (and, of course, adults) of the Grimm brothers' fairy tales is a powerful testament to the capacity of the moral tale to instil values and beliefs about people and the world. As Widdershoven and Smits point out, 'we can only hope to find adequate ways of dealing with ethical problems if we are prepared to listen to the narratives of the people involved . . . people constantly present themselves and their actions towards others by telling stories' (Widdershoven and Smits, 1996: 278–80). So not only can contributors' stories provide embodied examples of dual relationships, they can also convey the subtle tensions and complications of moral practice (McLeod, 2001; Price, 1996; White and Epston, 1992; Widdershoven and Smits, 1996). Moral matters cannot be solved purely by acts of reason, but also require psychological involvement and an intuitive connection with the topic (Widdershoven and Smits, 1996). The medium of story can be a vehicle through which we can develop a sense of intuitive connection with the landscape of complex relationships, as well as gather narrative exemplars through which we can learn and nurture our own approach. In addition, diverse cultural narratives can help us inform ourselves about relational differences and similarities that might well influence how we perceive and relate in complex relationship situations.

'Story' can powerfully both encourage and prohibit certain behaviours. As Botella et al. (2004: 119) argue, '[W]e live in (and through) stories, family myths, traditions and anecdotes.' According to Polkinghorne (2004: 59), socially acceptable story plots can provide meaning and value to our actions and interactions, that is, they can serve to encourage an original plot or storyline through promoting good actions, or alternatively, impede it through discouraging and inhibiting bad actions (Polkinghorne, 2004). For example, stories of complaints and litigation action, now commonplace in the US counselling profession, are powerful inhibitors for therapists contemplating entering into a dual relationship situation with a current or former client. A recent edited volume from Angus and McLeod (2004) provides a welcome resource through which to develop our understanding of narrative approaches in therapy.

In the process of reviewing draft chapters on client and practitioner experiences, some of the contributors offered further thoughts and I would like to include several comments here. One contributor noted the impact of misunderstanding person-centred therapy and highlighted the importance of robust and respectful theory that underpins sound practice.

> I do not know if there is more sloppy practice in person centred/humanistic therapy than in other theoretical orientation. From my personal experience, there is widespread misunderstanding of the robust theory underpinning sound person centred practice. It is now 4 years since the abusive therapy I was in broke down and I have had a positive experience of being in a healing therapy for 3 years. I can now look back and see clearly what went so terribly wrong – a dual relationship was just one example of the more general and abusive blurring of boundaries that began early on in the therapy.
>
> (A client-contributor)

This person's comment supports the notion that it is the 'person of the practitioner', as well as their capacity and intent in the relationship, that is crucial to the successful evolution of the ever-changing landscape and boundaries of a dual relationship.

One contributor's understanding of and practices in dual relationships had evolved since her original contribution, bringing with it the recognition of the complexity of the relationship.

> My present feelings about dual relationships in counselling are that they are on the one hand manageable and on the other complex. By this I mean, manageable in the sense of my being clear about boundaries and holding the separate issues that belong to different roles. This seems to work well. But complex in that beneath the surface of the relationship there always exists for me a sense of the other role. It is knowledge that cannot be unknown – and it shades or colours to some extent all encounters with the person with whom I have the dual relationship.

A client-contributor described how she approached reading the draft chapter on the client's experience with:

> a bit of anxiety, lest I felt disturbed again on reading my own and others' accounts of distress in this area. And yes, it did raise memories and feelings for me once more. I found it helpful to read of the experiences of others in that I felt less alone. It becomes a 'twinship' experience (Kohut), a sense of solidarity that there are others out there who have had similar experiences and felt the same way, both are important to me.

Another contributor expressed her concern that the people who shared their experiences with me should not be damaged by my use of their contribution. This goes straight to the paradoxical heart of the matter – how to share contributors' experiences in the public domain, while at the same time remaining faithful to the trust implicit in the researcher–participant relationship.

> Thank you for sending me your chapter . . . I found myself judgemental at what sometimes felt like a disastrous lack of awareness of the damage/potential damage that might be sustained by the client (not to mention the practitioner or the profession) as a consequence of some of the overlaps related. Yet I am aware of the problems people find themselves in as a consequence of working in an unsympathetic environment. I often felt incensed at the possibility that people's training had not prepared them for some of the most obvious boundary transgressions.

While the client and therapist contributors supported the research and many commented that much more on experiences of dual relationships needed to be available in the profession's literature, I did struggle with this and believe there is no easy resolution to this dilemma. My hope is that the completed text is respectful of the individuals who openly shared their stories.

Dual and multiple role-relating is tricky and sometimes perilous territory. Arguably, as a minimum, practitioner training should include the opportunity to think about and practise ethical problem-management skills to apply to dual relationships or similar complex relationship situations. As we have seen, the practitioner's role is pivotal, therefore their relational knowledge, skills and capacity are crucial. While we might assume that the majority of therapists are not intentionally abusive, we cannot take it for granted that they know how to respond to complex relational situations such as those found in many dual relationships. Consequently, I have key recommendations aimed largely at practitioner training, practice and supervision, although they do signify areas for further research and literature.

- Counsellor, supervisor and practitioner 'trainer training' should address the themes identified in this text. This should be done within the broad context of considering issues and features of complex relationships and form a central part of the training curriculum. This training experience would ideally incorporate role enactments as a means of fully exploring the relational phenomena being practised or experienced. In any subsequent situation of similar relational complexity, the practitioner will already have experienced this dramatic enactment and can use it to inform their thinking, decisions and actions/interactions. In addition, in their practices, practitioners might use a version of role enactment with clients in order to prepare or support them in situations of relational complexity – of the type likely to be encountered in dual and multiple overlapping roles. Exploring the range of knowledge, skills and abilities that will enable a therapist to ethically and competently deal with diversity and conflict in dual and multiple role-relating should be a mandatory curriculum subject in all core therapy training.
- Clients in dual and multiple role relationships need to be supported to deal with the relationship and the situations that they generate. This might take the form of mutual contracting sessions and reviews, clear practice information that outlines obligations and expectations of the roles of practitioner and client, or any of the other best practice strategies of therapists shown in the text.
- Practitioners must, through training at undergraduate and postgraduate level, be encouraged and facilitated to develop their decision-making and problem-management skills in order to deal with the type of complex, conflicted and contextualized situations presented by dual relationships and other complex relational situations.

- Relational ethics should be a central topic in all undergraduate and postgraduate-level training and should feature in Continuing Professional Development (CPD) programmes. Philosophical, ethical and pragmatic reasoning should constitute a central part of therapy training, perhaps phased over the duration of the practitioner's training and continuing into a post-practicum phase.
- The profession, through its professional bodies and training institutes, should consider the feasibility of introducing an obligatory postgraduate practicum period, during which time certain practice features and approaches to conceptualizing or dealing with the complex relational issues exemplified in dual relationships (among other ethical and professional challenges) are engaged within the context of closely supervised practice.

Clearly, we need to find non-exploitative, non-sexual ways to deal with dual relationships and think about how best to educate and encourage practitioners and their clients-dual relationship partners to think about the moral and ethical implications of their decisions and actions. Whether dual relationships are planned and desired, or unexpected and unwelcome, we appear to be at a point in the profession's development when it is time to legitimately and ethically question how those dual relationships that do occur can be best managed so that neither partner is harmed in the process. There must be many stories of beneficial or positively experienced dual relationships out there. For example, I recall one conference I attended where in conversation with a colleague they shared how they had successfully negotiated a dual relationship. They moved from a medium- to long-term practitioner–client relationship into a friendship relationship and because of their mutual agreement about the success of the relationship, they wondered about putting their story into the public domain. We need more examples of this kind.

We can legitimately question an unexamined ban on dual relationships and ask whether prohibition is realistic or even relevant in our contemporary multicultural society that espouses diversity, equal opportunity and human rights. It is time to consider when and how we might deem a dual relationship 'acceptable', as well as question how the partners could support and sustain themselves in the relationship. Given the significant evidence of the harmful potential of (some) dual relationships, it is not difficult to imagine how opposition to *all* dual relationships has evolved. However, as I argued earlier, the prohibitive situation and blanket ban are uncritically assumed and unrealistic in contemporary practice. Moreover, the changing structure of clinical roles as evidenced, for example, in NHS care contexts suggests that in a number of work settings, therapists will increasingly encounter clients in a range of roles. In order to move knowledge forward it is valid to appraise conventional wisdom, honour its contribution, question its continuing relevance and move on in an informed way, supported by the wisdom of our professional ancestors. In light of the evidence of the harmful outcome of some types of dual relationships (in particular, the evidence for the damaging affects of sexual dual relationships) I would argue that some proscriptions are necessary and valid.

We need to build on our research into and understanding of client and practitioner experiences of therapy relationships, processes and outcomes. To achieve this, we need detailed stories on being in dual relationships – from both a conceptual dimension and individuals' lived experiences. We also require systemic critiques of and inquiries into therapy in our constantly evolving multicultural and complex settings. A forthcoming edited volume on relational ethics in counselling and psychotherapy will go some way to address this (Gabriel and Casemore, forthcoming). Where dual relationships do occur, the therapist's role, as secular advisor or mentor, is to be a supportive and facilitative presence in the client's struggle to find ways of mediating the role conflicts and tensions in the various relationship roles. Where the counselling roles continue, there will be some types of dual relationships that are incompatible, or inadvisable.

At this point of completion and closure, I find myself wondering whether being in a dual relationship is less about questions of whether one should and more about matters of why and how one is. It certainly seems to be less a matter of abolishing or removing the relational issues and conflicts of complex relationships and more a case of learning how to ethically deal with the situation and develop increasingly sophisticated relational strategies. Essentially, it requires intricate ethical and moral manoeuvres through dense relational terrain. Although some dual relationships will be contra-indicated, from the evidence produced here I would argue that in some circumstances, non-sexual dual relationships can be a valuable, ethical and moral encounter – as was suggested by the experience of several of the clients and therapists. In addition, I find myself wanting to echo Jones's (2001: 289) sentiments to 'embrace, however uncomfortably and ambivalently, a passion for ignorance . . . [and] allow for the possibility of not-knowing'. There are many things unknown about these relationships at this stage in the profession's knowledge and understanding of human relationships. Recent developments in quantum physics suggest that multiple and complex dimensions co-exist in the universe (Ferguson, 2000; Greene, 1999), supporting the notion that we know far less about mediating the complexities of being in dual and multiple relationships than we might imagine. Nevertheless, we do know the harmful potential of dual relationships and need to ask whether we are up to the challenges we might face in this kind of relationship. If we are not, then how can we become so?

It is possible to construct a way through the challenges of a dual or multiple role relationship, but we need the sustenance of good supervision and sound thinking and practice – all based on firm foundations provided by quality training and supervision and supported by ongoing professional growth and development. Equally, we need the courage and good grace to know when to decline or end a dual relationship – in a humane and fitting way. Essentially, in the context of dual or multiple role relationship, we meet challenges that face all human relating. We might usefully consider the metaphor of becoming an ethics warrior; taking up our sword to courageously quest and clear a way through the unexplored or tangled thicket of the relational features confronting us, to the point of either finding a clear enough existing pathway, or forging another. Like all warriors, we tire; we cannot go on without sustenance and we need to replenish ourselves intellectually, spiritually and emotionally in order to undertake our quest. Clearly, our companions and co-warriors along the way (including our clients, supervisors and peers) are crucial resources. However, in the spirit of all questing, we face towards the unknown. We might draw strength and wisdom from previous warrior explorers, but we cannot avoid facing unknown territory, and thus must become a 'bricoleur'[1] warrior, forging a relational ethic as we ride the boundaries of being with one another.

---

1 Denzin and Lincoln (1998) liken the exploratory and constructive inquiry role to that of the bricoleur. The bricoleur is a skilled craftswoman or craftsman, creatively and thoughtfully seeking the most appropriate means and methods in order to form their work.

Appendix 1

SAMPLE QUESTIONS FOR ASSESSING DUAL AND MULTIPLE ROLE RELATIONSHIP SITUATIONS

The following questions arose from the clients' and practitioners' accounts of being in dual and multiple role relationships.

Questions to consider about the relationship
1. What are its defining feaures?
2. Is it circumstantial or unplanned?
3. Is it intended?
4. What is the duration and status of the therapy roles?
5. Is the dual relationship concurrent or sequential?
6. If it is concurrent, are the roles compatible?
7. What are the features, conditions and obligations of the various relationship roles?
8. How do they/might they interact?
9. What are the points of tension?
10. What do we regard as the primary role?
11. If the therapy relationship is ongoing, is it regarded as the primary relationship?
12. Will we know if/when/how to end the relationship?
13. What are the benefits and pitfalls of the relationship?
14. How can concerns, problems or conflicts be dealt with?
15. What happens post-termination – does the therapist continue to perceive the client as 'client'?
16. Where the therapy roles are historic, what (if any) unfinished business remains? For instance, what transferences or projections need to be resolved?

17. Is there evidence of potentially unhelpful features or dynamics in the relationship? For example, are there any hidden personal or professional agendas?
18. When the relationship is working well, what relational features and qualities might be evident? What is happening at an individual or interactive and relational level?

Questions to consider about the relational context
  1. How does the context(s) in which the relationship is played out interact with other factors in dual relationships?
  2. How can therapy and non-therapy contact and activities be separated? How can we work with boundaries to appropriately separate them?
  3. How can the boundaries be negotiated and set in place? How will they be monitored and reviewed?
  4. What are/are there cultural, or professional, or organizational norms and beliefs influencing the dual or multiple role relationship? How do they/might they affect the relationship?

Questions related to where it might be best (or most appropriate) to situate reviews or appraisals of dual relationships
  1. Where should a review take place? The therapy relationship? The overlapping roles? Both?
  2. What are the roles and responsibilities of a therapist's training institute, trainers and supervisors in helping the therapist learn how best to deal with dual relationships?
  3. What role or purpose does/can therapist training play in preparing practitioners for dealing with/learning how to deal with general duality issues and dual relationships? For example, how does/does training address the ethical and professional challenges presented by dual relationships?
  4. What role can/does undergraduate and postgraduate training and learning, as well as continuing personal and professional development, play?
  5. What role might supervision and/or training play in identifying and acknowledging the cultural, conceptual, theoretical and clinical features that might influence how the therapist works with the dual relationship and how the client experiences or perceives the relationship?

Questions associated with the role that theories and concepts play in constructing or influencing the relationship context
1. What theories, concepts and practices could influence or inform my/our relational decisions and actions?
2. What are their strengths and limitations?
3. How might they help or hinder my/our dealing with the dual relationship?

Questions about the client and practitioner
1. Is the dual relationship consensual? Are we both as aware as possible of the likely implications and consequences? What are my/her/his intentions in pursuing the additional roles?
2. Do past experiences or relationships with significant others influence how I/we enter into, relate and manage ourselves in the dual relationship and associated situations? If so, how?
3. What might prevent me/the client challenging or discussing the dual relationship with me or with someone else? What might prevent me (the therapist) challenging myself about the dual relationship, or discussing relationship issues or concerns with my supervisor or experienced therapy colleagues?
4. Might I/we be seeking deeper and extended contact through pursuing a dual relationship? Are we/am I afraid of losing the person/relationship for some reason?
5. Am I/are they sufficiently robust to sustain self in the dual relationship? Might I/we be withholding any reactions? If I encounter emotional or psychological problems arising from the relationship, how will I deal with them? Am I/we open to being challenged about the relationship? What support is available if difficulties arise?
6. What factors might prevent or hinder either of us from developing role literacy?
7. What is the my/their attachment style in past/present relationships? Assessing a person's relational style in therapy and non-therapy roles may provide an indication of their capacity to sustain themselves in the relationship, and in the case of the therapist, their capacity to also sustain the client
8. How might my/their personal history and previous relational experiences and preferences influence the process and outcome of the relationships?

9. Do I/we have any assumptions about one another, or any aspects of the various relationship roles that we share (this includes both expressed and unarticulated assumptions)?

10. Is there any personal conflict for me/her/him? How will I as therapist know whether and/or when supervisory consultation, personal therapy or some other type of personal/supportive intervention is appropriate or necessary? How will I/will I be able to recognize if, when, and on what grounds, a relationship should be terminated?

11. What are the interpersonal issues in this dual relationship? What interactions or situations do I/you/we find problematic or difficult?

12. How might your/my personality influence your/my perceptions and experiences, as well as responses in the dual relationship?

13. How might issues related to lack or loss of trust impact on the client?

14. Does the client in any way defer to the perceived power of the therapist?

15. What might prevent the client bringing their relational issues into the therapy relationship?

16. If therapy is ended, where else can issues be discussed? Is one of the dual or multiple roles more conducive to discussing the relationship?

17. How can I account for my relational decisions, actions and interventions with the client, with colleagues, in supervision, with a complaints tribunal?

18. What might help with developing the competence and confidence to deal with the complexities of a dual or multiple role relationship?

Appendix 2

GUIDANCE FOR ETHICAL DECISION-MAKING: A SUGGESTED MODEL FOR PRACTITIONERS*

Lynne Gabriel and Roger Casemore

Introduction

This practice guideline offers a decision-making process for thinking through ethical challenges or dilemmas. It is offered as a productive way of responding to ethical challenges or dilemmas. This guideline aims to provide guidance to practitioners and to support them in thinking through the ethical challenges they meet in their practice, so that actions they take are likely to be ethically justifiable to clients, the profession and society in general.

A process model for ethical decision-making

Whether the situations leading to an ethical dilemma arise from the 'what if' process or from an actual therapeutic relationship, decisions have to be made and the following has been found useful:

1. Stop, think and identify the situation or problem
2. Construct a description

* This is an adapted version of a practice guidance document written for BACP by L. Gabriel and R. Casemore, *The Ethical Decision Making Process: A Suggested Model for Practitioners*. Rugby: BACP, 2003).

3. Whose problem is it?
4. Review in terms of the BACP Ethical Framework
5. Consider moral principles and values
6. Identify the support that is available
7. Identify courses of action
8. Select a course of action
9. Evaluate the outcome
10. Regularly check the personal impact of the situation or events

1. Stop, think, identify the situation or problem

Stop, think, consider the facts and identify any feelings and initial thoughts about the situation. Check whether it is capable of resolution. It may be helpful to discuss this stage with a supervisor or an experienced colleague.

2. Construct a clear description of the situation or problem

This important initial step helps to clarify the situation and minimize confusion. It is especially helpful to have formulated an outline of the situation before discussing it with a supervisor or experienced counselling or psychotherapy colleague.

Essentially, this step of the process model identifies the contextual features of the issue or dilemma. For example, are there unique cultural, race, sexual identity, or other contextual features involved in the situation?

3. Whose problem is it?

(a) The practitioner?
(b) The client?
(c) A joint problem?
(d) An agency/organization problem?

Personal, professional and organizational features can all come into play and thus need to be considered in any decision-making processes. This step considers the 'players' involved and seeks to identify some of the relational features. Where there are complex relational features, consider questions such as:

(i)   Who is involved in the situation?
(ii)   Who are the main players and stakeholders?
(iii)   What personal and/or professional issues do they bring to the situation?
(iv)   What values, assumptions, attitudes are/appear to be prevailing?
(v)   What are the individual's roles/responsibilities/obligations/expectations?
(vi)   Are there any relevant contractual or legal matters underlying this conflict?
(vii)   How might these help/hinder the situation?
(viii) What are the individuals' perceptions of the situation?
(ix)   Might there be any unspoken or hidden motives?
(x)   What are the main points of tension, conflict or paradox?

Additionally, consider such questions as:

(xi)   What is/was my role in all of this?
(xii)   How have I contributed to the situation?
(xiii) What is the impact on my client and what is the impact on me?
(xiv)   Who can help me clarify and appraise my part in the situation?

Where joint or multiple responsibility for the situation exists, then roles, responsibilities and relationship boundaries need to be carefully considered, clarified and negotiated. The Information Sheet 'Working in a Multitasked Job' might be helpful. This document is available through BACP's Ethical Helpline or Information Office.

4. Review in terms of the BACP Ethical Framework

Consider all relevant sources of guidance including: BACP's Ethical Framework for Good Practice; appropriate Information Sheets and Guidelines for Good Practice; relevant legislation and literature. Consider, if appropriate:

(a) What actions are prohibited/required according to professional ethics and practice guidance?

(b)   What actions are prohibited/required by law?
(c)   What actions are required in this working context?
(d)   Reflect on these, and also consult with a supervisor or practice consultant.

Identify any possible conflicts between ethical principles and the law and take advice on these.

5. Consider moral principles and values

Moral principles provide a way of evaluating the critical relationship, context and stakeholder dimensions of a given ethical and professional issue or dilemma. Moral principles and values can compete or conflict and reaching a decision on an ethical or professional issue can demand considerable courage and commitment on the part of the practitioner. It is important that the practitioner can clearly account for any decisions reached and actions taken. Ultimately, the practitioner has to live with their decisions and actions and deal with any associated personal or professional consequences.

In the absence of decisive or definitive guidelines, consider the following principles:

- **Beneficence:** what decisions and actions will achieve the greatest good?
- **Non-maleficence:** what decisions and actions will cause the least harm?
- **Justice:** what decisions and actions will be fairest for all parties involved?
- **Autonomy:** what decisions and actions respect and maximize opportunities for individuals to implement their own reasoned and informed choices? For example, how capable are the client and the therapist of making free and informed choices?
- **Fidelity:** the client–practitioner relationship is a relationship that is based on the trust that the practitioner can be relied upon to provide an ethical and caring service. The notion of fidelity also brings into question the 'person of the practitioner', that is their personal and professional knowledge, skills and abilities, as well as their values and attitudes.

- **Self-respect:** fostering the practitioner's self-knowledge and care for self. The practitioner appropriately applies all of the above principles as entitlements for self.

6. Identify the support that is available

Identify who is available to offer support, guidance, or other types of help (for example, supervisor/supervisory consultant, colleagues, mentor, etc.); think about any other resources that can be drawn upon (e.g. BACP's Ethical Helpline).

7. Identify courses of action

Brainstorm possible courses of action. Consider as wide a range of options as possible. The options can be reviewed, reformulated or discarded as appropriate. Depending upon circumstances, this step will be carried out with the input, support and cooperation of the client/supervisor/experienced therapist colleague. Consider the impact and likely consequences of each action identified.

8. Select a course of action

Given the:
- contextual and relational features
- ethical and moral dimensions
- available literature
- consultation process with all involved in the situation
- review of the situation with supervisor(s) and therapy colleagues

(a) What is the best, most appropriate course of action on this occasion?
(b) What are the likely consequences of action or inaction, in the short, medium and long term?
(c) Consider what advice and guidance might be needed to help make a decision, and from whom. In addition, consider the chosen course of action against the following:

(a) Justification

How would decisions be accounted for with:

(i)   The client?
(ii)   Myself?
(iii)   My supervisor(s)?
(iv)   My professional peers, colleagues?
(v)   My employing organisation(s)?
(vi)   A complaints tribunal?
(vii)   A court of law?
(viii) The media?

(b) Universality

(i)   For example, could a chosen course of action be recommended to others?
(ii)   Would the chosen actions be condoned if a colleague were to follow the same course?
(iii)   Would the same course of action be taken with another client or in another context?
(iv)   If the client were famous or influential, would the decisions be the same, or different?
(v)   If different, 'why' and 'how' would they differ?

Consider the consequences of each action using the 'What if . . .' process.

9. Evaluate the outcome

When reviewing and assessing the outcome of decisions and actions, consider the following:

(a) Was the outcome as imagined or hoped for, or expected?
(b) Had all relevant factors been considered with the result that no new, or surprising, factors emerged?
(c) Would the same course of action be taken in the future?
(d) Feedback should be sought from a supervisor and colleagues asking them to suggest what, if anything, might have been done differently
(e) If **the answer to any of these is no**, consider what could be done differently should the situation arise again.

10. Regularly check the personal impact of the situation or events

- throughout the decision-making process, practitioners should remember to check out from time to time how the situation is affecting them;
- check out whether the situation has identified any skills or knowledge areas that need to be developed;
- depending on the impact of the situation, it might be useful to consider personal therapy.
  (*Source*: adapted from Bond, 2000; Gabriel, 1996, 2000b)

Concluding comments

The ideas presented here are neither radical nor daunting – they simply invite and encourage practitioners to mobilize and develop their capacity for good-quality work and to place client protection at the centre of helping relationships. Most practitioners are ethically literate (Gabriel, 2001a) but might not recognize or acknowledge the resources they have or, more importantly, those they lack. With the introduction of BACP's Ethical Framework, the profession is maturing and relying less on paternalistic dictates and more on an ethical framework that both acknowledges the potential of the practitioner and safeguards the interests of the client. Practitioners can now branch out from the secure base set down by several decades of good guidance provided by earlier versions of detailed codes of practice. Clearly, new and inexperienced individuals are always entering this changing profession, and may join at a point where they are not sufficiently competent or confident to interpret and formulate ethical practice. Here, good-quality training and supervision will be crucial, complemented by decision-making models to aid thinking and practice.

The framework constitutes a reflexive and pragmatic approach to dealing with ethical and moral issues. This approach can help to contain some of the chaos and conflict that can be present in problematic situations. It can be used when working alone, or in consultation with supervisors or colleagues. Clearly, the more complex the ethical issue, the greater the need for supervisory or consultative support.

Case study

The following case study shows how the model might be brought into a practice context:

1. *What if . . .* my clients live in the same small town as me and we find ourselves sharing social and recreational facilities?

Sally was a recently qualified counsellor who lived and worked in the same small town as many of her clients and she often encountered them at shared social and recreational venues, or contexts such as the local GP's or dentist's waiting room. She worked part-time as a counsellor in the local GP surgery and wanted to develop a small private practice. Sally valued her social life and did not want either herself or her partner to miss events and activities that they both enjoyed. For example, they both were keen bowlers and she would often see current and former clients at the local bowling club. She felt uncomfortable about the range of reactions she received from some of her clients about this overlapping contact, as well as from several of her city colleagues who saw it as unprofessional. A few of her clients appeared to be very embarrassed about seeing her in contexts other than the therapy room. Some wanted to seek her out when they met in social settings and this could be problematic when she was with family and friends. She decided to discuss the situation with her supervisor.

(*Source*: adapted from Gabriel and Casemore, 2003)

In relation to considering this situation against the decision-making model, Sally realized that the overlapping therapy and non-therapy contact was problematic for some clients, so was aware that the situation might become ethically challenging. In this case, then, step 1 ('stop and identify the situation or problem') appears to be a matter of recognizing a situation of potentially tricky dual or multiple role relationships.

Sally constructed a description of the situation (step 2) in order to be able to discuss it more clearly in supervision. With regard to 'whose problem is it' (step 3), Sally thought it was a problem for both herself and her clients. The clients had varying reactions to meeting her outside therapy, while she had to deal with her partner's questions about the individuals, as well as her own feelings about being witnessed by her clients in situations where she wanted to 'let her hair down'. Before meeting with her supervisor, Sally briefly scanned BACP's Ethical Framework (2002) to see if she could find any guidance on her situation (step 4 and 5). On page 4 of this document, it stated that:

> [D]ual relationships arise when the practitioner has two or more kinds of relationship concurrently with a client . . . The existence of a dual relationship with a client is seldom neutral and can have a powerful beneficial or detrimental impact that may not always be easily foreseeable. For these reasons practitioners are required to consider the implications of entering into dual relationships with clients, to avoid entering into relationships that are likely to be detrimental to clients, and to be readily accountable to clients and colleagues for any dual relationships that occur.

Although this was clear, Sally did not feel that she was any clearer about how to respond in the situation. She re-read the rest of the document and considered the situation against some of the moral principles that were noted: (1) *beneficence* (promoting the client's well-being); she considered, for example, questions such as 'by being in other types of relationships with my clients, how am I promoting their well-being?' 'does this promote or inhibit their well-being?'; (2) *non-maleficence* (avoid harming the client) – she was not too sure about this principle, since she felt that one or two of the clients might actually be having difficulty with the overlapping roles; she decided that she needed to explore this in supervision; (3) *autonomy* (respecting the client's right to be self-governing) – she also wondered about this principle, since she had not discussed the overlapping contact with clients and had assumed that they were ok about it; although she felt it would be difficult to admit to her supervisor that she was having doubts and encountering problems around the overlapping contacts, she decided she would discuss this with her supervisor; (4) *fidelity* (honouring the trust that the client places in the practitioner) – she wondered whether and how the social and recreational contact compromised the confidentiality promised to clients; (5) self-respect (fostering the practitioner's self-knowledge and care for self) – she explored the impact on self in supervision. She also scanned the section headed 'Guidance on Good Practice in Counselling and Psychotherapy' and decided that there were several areas of her practice being called into question; especially in relation to providing good-quality care and keeping trust in the client relationships.

The more she thought about the situation, the more complex it became and she realized that she needed the support of her supervisor to help her explore the situation and its various dimensions (step 6). Sally explored the remaining steps of the model in her supervision (that is, identifying and selecting an appropriate course of action, evaluating her choice and reviewing the impact of the situation on her, both personally and professionally). From her reflections and explorations in supervision, as well as discussions with her clients, Sally was able to identify ways of managing the overlapping therapy and non-therapy contacts. Most of her clients found the discussions about dealing with the overlapping role boundaries and how to be with one another in non-therapy contexts very helpful. For those clients who found it more difficult to deal with the situation, by clearly talking things through with the client, as well as using her supervision to clarify her thinking, interventions and actions, she found other ways of responding. For instance, in some cases, it was possible to agree and arrange ways of her or the client avoiding certain venues.

FURTHER READING FOR ETHICAL DECISION-MAKING MODELS

Betan, E.J. (1997). Toward a Hermeneutic Model of Ethical Decision Making in Clinical Practice. *Ethics & Behavior* 7, 347–65.

Cottone, R.R. and Claus, R.E. (2000). Ethical Decision-Making Models: A Review of the Literature. *Journal of Counseling and Development* 78, 3, 275–83.

Gabriel, L. and Davies, D. (2000). The Management of Ethical Dilemmas Associated with Dual Relationships. In *Pink Therapy, Vol. 3: Issues in Therapy with Lesbian, Gay, Bisexual and Transgendered Clients*, ed. Neal, C. and Davies, D., pp. 35–54. Buckingham: Open University Press.

Hill, M., Glaser, K. and Harden, J. (1995). A Feminist Model for Ethical Decision Making. In *Ethical Decision Making in Therapy*, ed. Rave, E.J.R. and Larsen, C.C.L., pp. 18–37. New York: Guilford Press.

Robson, M., Cook, P., Hunt, K., Aldred, G. and Robson, D. (2000). Towards Ethical Decision-Making in Counselling Research. *British Journal of Guidance & Counselling* 28, 4, 533–48.

Sherwin, S. (2001). Feminist Reflections on the Role of Theories in a

Global Bioethics. In *Globalizing Feminist Ethics*, ed. Tong, R., Anderson, G. and Santos, A., pp. 12–26. Boulder, CO: Westview Press.

GENERAL REFERENCES ON ETHICS

Beauchamp. T.L. and Childress, J.F. (1994). *Principles of Biomedical Ethics* (4th edn). New York: Oxford University Press.

Bond, T. (1993). *Standards and Ethics for Counselling in Action*. London: Sage.

Bond, T. (2000). *Standards and Ethics for Counselling in Action* (2nd edn). London: Sage.

British Association for Counselling and Psychotherapy (2002). *Ethical Framework for Good Practice in Counselling and Psychotherapy*. Rugby: BACP.

Casemore, R. (1999). The Paradoxical Nature of Feelings. *Counselling and Psychotherapy Journal* 11, 5, 278.

Casemore, R. (2001). *Surviving Complaints against Counsellors and Psychotherapists: Understanding and Healing the Hurt*. Manchester: PCCS Books.

Clarkson, P. (2000). *Ethics: Working with Ethical and Moral Dilemmas in Psychotherapy*. London: Whurr.

Gabriel, L. (2001a). A Matter of Ethical Literacy. *Counselling and Psychotherapy Journal* 12, 6, 14–15.

Gabriel, L. (2001b). Speaking the Unspeakable: Dual Relationships in Counselling and Psychotherapy. Unpublished doctoral thesis. York St John, a college of the University of Leeds, UK.

Gottlieb, M.C. (1993). Avoiding Exploitative Dual Relationships: A Decision-Making Model. *Psychotherapy* 30, 41–8.

Jones, C., Shilloto-Clarke, C., Syme, G., Hill, D., Casemore, R. and Murdin, L. (2000). *Questions of Ethics in Counselling and Therapy*. Buckingham: Open University Press.

Kitchener, K.S. (1984). Intuition, Critical Evaluation and Ethical Principles: The Foundation for Ethical Decisions for Counselling Psychology. *The Counseling Psychologist* 12, 3, 43–55.

Meara, N.M., Schmidt, L.D. and Day, J.D. (1996). Principles and Virtues: A Foundation for Ethical Decisions, Policies, and Character. *The Counseling Psychologist* 24, 1, 4–77.

Palmer Barnes, F. and Murdin, L. (eds) (2001). *Values and Ethics in the Practice of Psychotherapy and Counselling*. Buckingham: Open University Press.

Pope, K.S. and Vasquez, M.J.T. (1998). *Ethics in Psychotherapy and Counseling* (2nd edn). San Francisco: Jossey-Bass.

Other related resources can be found at www.advocate.com

Appendix 3

USEFUL CONTACTS

British Association for Counselling and Psychotherapy (BACP)
BACP House
35–37 Albert Street
Rugby
Warwickshire
CV21 2SG
Telephone: 0870 4435252
Website: www.bacp.co.uk

British Psychological Society (BPS)
St Andrew's House
48 Princess Road East
Leicester
LE1 7DR
Telephone: 0116 2549568
Website: www.bps.org.uk

Prevention of Professional Abuse Network (POPAN)
1 Wyvil Court
Wyvil Road
London
SW8 2TG
Telephone: 020 76226334
Website: www.popan.org.uk

United Kingdom Council for Psychotherapy (UKCP)
167–169 Great Portland Street
London
W1N 5FB
Telephone: 020 74363002
Website: www.psychotherapy.org.uk

Bibliography

Almond, B. (1998). *Exploring Ethics: A Traveller's Tale*. Oxford: Blackwell.

American Psychiatric Association (2000). *Diagnostic and Statistical Manual of Mental Disorders* (text revision). Washington, DC: Author.

Anderson, S.K. and Davies, T.G. (2000). An Ethical Decision-Making Model: A Necessary Tool for Community College Presidents and Boards of Trustees. *Community College Journal of Research and Practice* 24, 9, 711–27.

Angus, L. and McLeod, J. (eds) (2004). *The Handbook of Narrative and Psychotherapy: Practice, Theory, and Research*. London: Sage.

Backlar, P. (1996). The Three Rs: Roles, Relationships, and Rules. *Community Mental Health Journal* 32, 5, 505–9.

Baer, B.E. and Murdock, N.L. (1995). Nonerotic Dual Relationships Between Therapists and Clients: The Effects of Sex, Theoretical Orientation, and Interpersonal Boundaries. *Ethics and Behavior* 5, 2, 131–45.

Baker, E.K. (2003). *Caring for Ourselves: A Therapist's Guide to Personal and Professional Well-Being*. Washington, DC: American Psychological Association.

Barnet, J.E. (1996). Boundary Issues and Dual Relationships: Where to Draw the Line? *The Independent Practitioner* 16, 3, 138–40.

Beauchamp. T.L. and Childress, J.F. (1994). *Principles of Biomedical Ethics* (4th edn). New York: Oxford University Press.

Betan, E.J. (1997). Toward a Hermeneutic Model of Ethical Decision Making in Clinical Practice. *Ethics & Behavior* 7, 4, 347–65.

Beutler, L.E., Machado, P.P.P. and Neufeldt, S.A. (1994). Therapist Variables. In *Handbook of Psychotherapy and Behaviour Change* (4th edn), ed. Bergin, A.E. and Garfield, S.L., pp. 229–69. New York: John Wiley.

Bond, T. (1997). Therapists' Dilemmas as Stimuli to New Understanding and Practice. In *Therapists' Dilemmas* (revised edition) ed. Dryden, W. London: Sage.

Bond, T. (2000). *Standards and Ethics for Counselling in Action* (2nd edn). London: Sage.

Bordin, E.S. (1979). The Generalizability of the Psychoanalytic Concept of the Working Alliance. *Psychotherapy: Theory, Research and Practice* 16, 252–60.

Bordin, E. S. (1994). Theory and Research on the Therapeutic Working Alliance: New Directions. In *The Working Alliance: Theory, Research, and Practice*, ed. Horvath, A.O. and Greenberg, L. New York: John Wiley & Sons.

Borys, D.S. and Pope, K.S. (1989). Dual Relationships between Therapist and Client: A National Study of Psychologists, Psychiatrists and Social Workers. *Professional Psychology: Research and Practice* 20, 5, 283–93.

Botella, L., Herrero, O., Pacheco, M. and Corbella, S. (2004). In *The Handbook of Narrative and Psychotherapy: Practice, Theory, and Research*, ed. Angus, L. and McLeod, J., pp. 119–36. Thousand Oaks, CA: Sage.

Bowlby, J. (1969). *Attachment and Loss, 2 vols, Volume 1: Attachment*. London: Hogarth Press.

Bowlby, J. (1979). *The Making and Breaking of Affectional Bonds*. London: Tavistock Publications.

British Association for Counselling (BAC) (1998). *Code of Ethics and Practice for Counsellors*. Rugby: BAC.

British Association for Counselling and Psychotherapy (BACP) (2002). *Ethical Framework for Good Practice in Counselling and Psychotherapy*. Rugby: BACP.

British Psychological Society (BPS) (1997). *Code of Conduct, Ethical Principles & Guidelines*. Leicester: BPS.

Brown, L.S. (1991). Antiracism as an Ethical Imperative: An Example for Feminist Therapy. *Ethics & Behavior* 1, 2, 69–86.

Brown, L.S. (1994). *Subversive Dialogues: Theory in Feminist Therapy*. New York: Basic Books.

Browne, R.B. (ed.) (1984). *Forbidden Fruits: Taboos and Tabooism in Culture*. Bowling Green University, OH: Bowling Green University Popular Press.

Buber, M. (1937). *I and Thou*. Trans. Kaufmann, K. New York: Charles Scribner.

Cashdan, S. (1988). *Object Relations Therapy: Using the Relationship*. New York: W.W. Norton.

Celenza, A. and Hilsenroth, M. (1997). Personality Characteristics of Mental Health Professionals Who have Engaged in Sexualized Dual Relationships: A Rorschach Investigation. *Bulletin of the Menninger Clinic* 61, 1, 90–107.

Chaplin, J. (1988). *Feminist Counselling in Action*. London: Sage.

Chase, S.E. (1996). Personal Vulnerability and Interpretive Authority in

Narrative Research. In *The Narrative Study of Lives: Ethics and Process in the Narrative Study of Lives*, ed. Josselson, R., pp. 45–59. Thousand Oaks, CA: Sage.

Clarkson, P. (1994). In Recognition of Dual Relationships. *Transactional Analysis Journal* 24, 1, 32–8.

Clarkson, P. (1995). *The Therapeutic Relationship*. London: Whurr.

Clarkson, P. (2000). *Ethics: Working with Ethical and Moral Dilemmas in Psychotherapy*. London: Whurr.

Clarkson, P. (2002). *The Transpersonal Relationship in Psychotherapy*. London: Whurr.

Clarkson, P. and Murdin, L. (1996). When Rules are Not Enough: The Spirit of the Law in Ethical Codes. *Counselling* 8, 31–35.

Cole, M. (1988). Sex Therapy for Individuals. In *Sex Therapy in Britain*, ed. Cole, M. and Dryden, W., pp. 272–99. Milton Keynes: Open University Press.

Coleman, E. and Schaefer, S. (1986). Boundaries of sex and intimacy between client and counselor. *Journal of Counseling and Development* 64, 5, 341–4.

Corey, G., Corey, M.S. and Callanan, P. (1993). *Issues and Ethics in the Helping Professions* (4th edn). Pacific Grove, CA: Brooks/Cole.

Corey, G., Corey, M.S. and Callanan, P. (2003). *Issues and Ethics in the Helping Professions* (6th edn). Pacific Grove, CA: Brooks/Cole.

Cottone, R.R. and Claus, R.E. (2000). Ethical Decision-Making Models: A Review of the Literature. *Journal of Counseling and Development* 78, 3, 275–83.

Coyle, A. (1998). Qualitative Research in Counselling Psychology: Using the Counselling Interview as a Research Instrument. In *Counselling Psychology: Integrating Theory, Research and Supervised Practice*, ed. P. Clarkson. London: Routledge.

Denzin, N.K. and Lincoln, Y.S. (1998). *The Landscape of Qualitative Research: Theories and Issues*. London: Sage.

Dickenson, D. (1991). *Moral Luck in Medical Ethics and Practical Politics*. Aldershot: Avebury.

Dryden, W. (ed.) (1987). *Key Cases in Psychotherapy*. London: Croom Helm.

Eatock, J. (2000). Counselling in Primary Care: Past, Present and Future. *British Journal of Guidance and Counselling* 28, 2, 161–73.

Edelwich, J. and Brodsky, A. (1991). *Sexual Dilemmas for the Helping Professional*. (2nd edn). New York: Bruner-Mazel.

Elliott, M. and Williams, D. (2003). The Client Experience of Counselling and Psychotherapy. *Counselling Psychology Review* 18, 1, 34–8.

Etherington, K. (1996). The Counsellor as Researcher: Boundary Issues and Critical Dilemmas. *British Journal of Guidance and Counselling* 24, 3, 339–46.

Etherington, K. (2000). *Narrative Approaches to Working with Adult Male Survivors of Child Sexual Abuse: The Client's, the Counsellor's and the Researcher's Story*. London: Jessica Kingsley.

Feltham, C. (ed.) (2000a). *Understanding the Counselling Relationship*. London: Sage.

Feltham, C. (2000b). Contextualising the Therapeutic Relationship. In *Understanding the Counselling Relationship*, ed. Feltham, C., pp. 4–32. London: Sage.

Ferguson, K. (2000). *Measuring the Universe: The Historical Quest to Quantify Space*. London: Hodder.

Finkelhor, D. (1986). *A Source Book on Child Sexual Abuse*. London: Sage.

Fish, B. and Dudas, K. (1999). The Relevance of Attachment Research for Adult Narratives Told in Psychotherapy. *Clinical Social Work Journal* 27, 1, 27–40.

Freud, S. (1962). *Two Short Accounts of Psycho-Analysis: Five Lectures on Psycho-Analysis and The Questions of Lay Analysis*. Hardmondsworth: Penguin.

Gabbard, G.O. (ed.) (1989). *Sexual Exploitation in Professional Relationships*. Washington, DC: American Psychiatric Press.

Gabriel, L. (1996). Boundaries in Lesbian Counsellor–Lesbian Client Relationships. Unpublished MEd. manuscript. York St John: York.

Gabriel, L. (1998). Materials presented at ALGBP-UK (Association for Lesbian, Gay, and Bisexual Psychology) Annual Training Conference. 7 March.

Gabriel, L. (1999). Practitioner–Researcher Role Conflict. Paper presented at BAC Research Conference. Leeds, UK.

Gabriel, L. (2000a). Dual Relationships in Organizational Contexts. *Counselling* 11, 1, 17–19.

Gabriel, L. (2000b). A Model for Working with Ethical Decion-Making and Problem-Solving. Materials presented to the Ethical Helpline Team, BACP.

Gabriel, L. (2001a). A Matter of Ethical Literacy. *Counselling and Psychotherapy Journal* 12, 6, 14–15.

Gabriel, L. (2001b). *Working in a Multitask Job*. Rugby: BACP.

Gabriel, L. (2001c). Speaking the Unspeakable: Dual Relationships in Counselling and Psychotherapy. Unpublished doctoral thesis. York St John College, York, UK.

Gabriel, L. and Casemore, R. (2003). *The Ethical Decision Making Process: A Suggested Model for Practitioners*. Rugby: BACP.

Gabriel, L. and Casemore, R. (forthcoming). *Relational Ethics in Counselling and Psychotherapy*.

Gabriel, L. and Davies, D. (2000). The Management of Ethical Dilemmas Associated with Dual Relationships. In *Pink Therapy, Vol. 3: Issues in*

Therapy with Lesbian, Gay, Bisexual and Transgendered Clients, ed. Neal, C. and Davies, D., pp. 35–54. Buckingham: Open University Press.

Garfield, S.L. (1994). Research on Client Variables in Psychotherapy. In *Handbook of Psychotherapy and Behavior Change* (4th edn), ed. Bergin, A.E. and Garfield, S.L., pp. 190–228. New York: John Wiley and Sons.

Gergen, K.J. and Kaye, J. (1992). Beyond Narrative in the Negotiation of Therapeutic Meaning. In *Therapy as Social Construction*, ed. McNamee, S. and Gergen, K.J., pp. 166–85. London: Sage.

Gilligan, C. (1982). *In A Different Voice: Psychological Theory and Women's Development*. Cambridge, MA: Harvard University Press.

Goffman, E. (1959). *The Presentation of Self in Everyday Life*. Garden City, NY: Doubleday.

Gottlieb, M.C. (1993). Avoiding Exploitative Dual Relationships: A Decision-Making Model. *Psychotherapy* 30, 41–8.

Grafanaki, S. (1996). How Research can Change the Researcher: The Need for Sensitivity, Flexibility and Ethical Boundaries in Conducting Qualitative Research in Counselling/Psychotherapy. *British Journal of Guidance and Counselling* 24, 329–38.

Gray, A. (1994) *An Introduction to the Therapeutic Frame*. London: Routledge.

Greene, B. (1999). *The Elegant Universe: Superstrings, Hidden Dimensions, and the Quest for the Ultimate Theory*. London: Jonathan Cape.

Greenson, R.R. (1967). *The Technique and Practice of Psychoanalysis*. Vol. 1. New York: International Universities Press.

Greenspan, M. (1993). On Professionalism. In *When Boundaries Betray Us: Beyond Illusions of What is Ethical in Therapy and Life*, ed. Heyward, C., pp. 193–205. San Francisco, CA: Harper Collins.

Gross, R. (1997) Attachment Theory: Extensions and Applications. *Psychology Review* 4, 2, 10–13.

Gutheil, T.G. and Gabbard, G.O. (1993). The Concept of Boundaries in Clinical Practice: Theoretical and Risk-Management Dimensions. *American Journal of Psychiatry* 150, 2, 188–96.

Gutheil, T.G. and Gabbard, G.O. (1995). Patient–Therapist Boundary Issues: An Integrative Review of Theory and Research. *Professional Psychology: Research and Practice* 26, 5, 499–506.

Handy, C.B. (1993). *Understanding Organizations* (3rd edn). Harmondsworth: Penguin.

Harding, S. (ed.) (1987). *Feminism & Methodology*. Milton Keynes: Open University Press.

Hart, N. and Crawford-Wright, A. (1999). Research as Therapy, Therapy as Research: Ethical Dilemmas in New-Paradigm Research. *British Journal of Guidance and Counselling* 27, 2, 205–14.

Hazan, C. and Shaver, P. (1987). Romantic Love Conceptualised as an Attachment Process. *Journal of Personality and Social Psychology* 52, 3, 511–24.

Heard, D. and Lake, B. (1997). *The Challenge of Attachment for Caregiving*. London: Routledge.

Hedges, L.E. (1997). In Praise of Dual Relationships. In *Therapists at Risk: Perils of the Intimacy of the Therapeutic Relationship*, ed. Hedges, L.E., Hilton, R., Hilton, V.W. and Candill, O.B., pp. 221–50. Northvale, NJ: Jason Aronson.

Herlihy, B. and Corey, G. (1992) *Dual Relationships in Counseling*. Alexandria, VA: American Counseling Association.

Heyward, C. (ed.) (1993). *When Boundaries Betray Us: Beyond Illusions of What is Ethical in Therapy and Life*. San Francisco, CA: Harper Collins.

Hill, M., Glaser, K. and Harden, J. (1995). A Feminist Model for Ethical Decision Making. In *Ethical Decision Making in Therapy*, ed. Rave, E.J.R. and Larsen, C.C.L., pp. 18–37. New York: Guildford Press.

Holmes, J. (1993). *John Bowlby and Attachment Theory*. London: Routledge.

Holmes, J. (1996). *Attachment, Intimacy, Autonomy: Using Attachment Theory in Adult Psychotherapy*. Northvale, NJ: Jason Aronson.

Holmes, J. (1997a). 'Too Early, Too Late': Endings in Psychotherapy: An Attachment Perspective. *British Journal of Psychotherapy* 14, 2, 159–71.

Holmes, J. (1997b). Attachment, Autonomy, Intimacy: Some Clinical Implications of Attachment Theory. *British Journal of Medical Psychology* 70, 3, 231–48.

Holmes, J. (2000). The Relationship in Psychodynamic Counselling. In *Understanding the Counselling Relationship*, ed. Feltham, C., pp. 33–54. London: Sage.

Holmes, J. (2001). *The Search for the Secure Base: Attachment Theory and Psychotherapy*. Hove: Brunner-Routledge.

Holmes, J. and Lindley, R. (1991). *The Values of Psychotherapy*. Oxford: Oxford University Press.

Horowitz, M.J. (1988). *Introduction to Psychodynamics: A New Synthesis*. London: Routledge.

Horvath, A.O. (1994). Empirical Validation of Bordin's Pantheoretical Model of the Alliance: The Working Alliance Inventory Perspective. In *The Working Alliance: Theory, Research, and Practice*, ed. Horvath, A.O. and Greenberg, L.S. New York: John Wiley & Sons.

Horvath, A.O. and Greenberg, L.S. (eds) (1994). *The Working Alliance: Theory, Research, and Practice*. New York: John Wiley & Sons.

ITA (Institute for Transactional Analysis) (1998). *Code of Professional Practice and Guidelines for Professional Practices*. London: ITA.

Jones, A. (2001). Cross-Cultural Pedagogy and the Passion for Ignorance. *Feminism & Psychology* 11, 3, 279–92.

Jones, C., Shilloto-Clarke, C., Syme, G., Hill, D., Casemore, R. and Murdin, L. (2000). *Questions of Ethics in Counselling and Therapy.* Buckingham: Open University Press.

Josselson, R. (ed.) (1996). *Ethics and Process in the Narrative Study of Lives.* Thousand Oaks, CA: Sage.

Kagle, J.D. and Giebelhausen, P.N. (1994). Dual Relationships and Professional Boundaries. *Social Work: Journal of the National Association of Social Workers* 39, 2, 213–19.

Kaufman, G. and Raphael, L. (1984). Shame as Taboo in American Culture. In *Forbidden Fruits: Taboos and Tabooism in Culture*, ed. Browne, R.B., pp. 57–66. Bowling Green, OH: Bowling Green University Popular Press.

Kennard, D. (1998). Personal Communication.

Khan, M. (1997). *Between Therapist and Client: The New Relationship* (revised edn). New York: Freeman and Company.

Kitchener, K.S. (1984). Intuition, Critical Evaluation and Ethical Principles: The Foundation for Ethical Decisions for Counseling Psychology. *The Counseling Psychologist* 12, 3, 43–55.

Kitchener, K.S. (1988). Dual Role Relationships: What Makes Them So Problematic? *Journal of Counseling and Development* 67, 4, 217–21.

Koehn, D. (1998). *Rethinking Feminist Ethics: Care, Trust and Empathy.* London: Routledge.

Krebs, R. (1980). Why Pastors should not be Counselors. *The Journal of Pastoral Care* 34, 229–33.

Landy, R.J. (1993). *Persona and Performance: The Meaning of Role in Drama, Therapy and Everyday Life.* London: Jessica Kingsley.

Landy, R.J. (1996). *Essays in Drama Therapy: The Double Life.* London: Jessica Kingsley.

Langs, R.J. (1976). *The Technique of Psychoanalytic Psychotherapy. Volume One.* New York: Jason Aronson.

Langs, R.J. (1978). *The Listening Process.* New York: Jason Aronson.

Langs, R.J. (1982). *The Psychotherapeutic Conspiracy.* New York: Jason Aronson.

Langs, R.J. (1988). *A Primer of Psychotherapy.* New York: Jason Aronson.

Langs, R.J. (2004). *The Fundamentals of Adaptive Psychotherapy in Psychotherapy.* Basingstoke, UK: Palgrave Macmillan.

Lazarus, A.A. (2001). Not all 'Dual Relationships' are Taboo; Some Tend to Enhance Treatment Outcomes. *The National Psychologist.* http:// national psychologist.com/articles/art_v9n7_1.htm (accessed 21/6/01).

Lazarus, A.A. and Zur, O. (eds) (2002). *Dual Relationships in Psychotherapy.* New York: Springer Publishing Co.

Lewin, K. (1948). *Resolving Social Conflicts: Selected Papers on Group Dynamics.* New York: Harper & Row.

Lindsay, G. and Clarkson, P. (1999). Ethical Dilemmas of Psychotherapists. *The Psychologist* 12, 3, 182–5.

McCartney, J. (1966). Overt Transference. *Journal of Sex Research* 2, 227–37.

McGrath, G. (1994). Ethics, Boundaries, and Contracts: Applying Moral Principles. *Transactional Analysis Journal* 24, 1, 6–14.

McLeod, J. (1997). *Narrative and Psychotherapy*. London: Sage.

McLeod, J. (1998). *An Introduction to Counselling* (2nd edn). Buckingham: Open University Press.

McLeod, J. (1999a). *Practitioner Research in Counselling*. London: Sage.

McLeod. J. (1999b). The Concept of the Story in Counselling and Psychotherapy: A Hermeneutic Approach. *Changes* 17, 3, 171–7.

McLeod, J. (2001). *Qualitative Research in Counselling and Psychotherapy*. London: Sage.

McNamee, S. and Gergen, K.J. (eds) (1992). *Therapy as Social Construction*. London: Sage.

McNamee, S. and Gergen, K.J. (eds) (1999). *Relational Responsibility: Resources for Sustainable Dialogue*. Thousand Oaks, CA: Sage.

MacKay, E. and O'Neill, P. (1992). What Creates the Dilemma in Ethical Dilemmas? Examples from Psychological Practice. *Ethics and Behavior* 2, 4, 227–44.

Main, M., Kaplan, N. and Cassidy, J. (1985). Security in Infancy, Childhood and Adulthood: A Move to the Level of Representation. In *Growing Points of Attachment Theory and Research*, ed. Bretherton, I. and Walters, E., pp. 66–104. Monographs of the Society for Research in Child Development, 50 (1–2, Serial No. 209).

Mallinckrodt, B., Coble, H.M. and Gantt, D.L. (1995). Toward Differentiating Client Attachment from Working Alliance and Transference: A Reply to Robbins. *Journal of Counseling Psychology* 42, 3, 320–2.

Mallinckrodt, B., Gantt, D.L. and Coble, H.M. (1995). Attachment Patterns in the Psychotherapy Relationship: Development of the Client Attachment to Therapist Scale. *Journal of Counseling Psychology* 42, 3, 307–17.

Mann, D. (1999). *Erotic Transference and Countertransference: Clinical Practice in Psychotherapy*. London: Routledge.

Mann, D. (2001). Erotics and Ethics: The Passionate Dilemmas of the Therapeutic Couple. In *Values and Ethics in the Practice of Psychotherapy and Counselling*, ed. Palmer Barnes, F. and Murdin, L., pp. 63–81. Buckingham: Open University Press.

Masson, J. (1985) *The Assault on Truth*. Penguin: Harmondsworth.

Meara, N.M., Schmidt, L.D. and Day, J.D. (1996). Principles and Virtues: A Foundation for Ethical Decisions, Policies, and Character. *The Counseling Psychologist* 24, 1, 4–77.

Mearns, D. (1997). *Person-Centred Counselling Training*. London: Sage.

Mearns, D. (2003). *Developing Person-Centred Counselling* (2nd edn). London: Sage.

Mearns, D. and Thorne, B. (2000). *Person-Centred Therapy Today: New Frontiers in Theory and Practice*. London: Sage.

Montgomery, M.J. and DeBell, C. (1997). Dual Relationships in Pastoral Counseling: Asset or Liability? *Counseling and Values* 42, 1, 30–40.

Moreno, J.L. (1947). *The Theatre of Spontaneity*. Beacon, NY: Beacon House.

Morgan, S. (1996). *Helping Relationships in Mental Health*. London: Chapman & Hall.

Neal, C. and Davies, D (eds) (2000). *Pink Therapy, Vol. 3: Issues in Therapy with Lesbian, Gay, Bisexual and Transgendered Clients*. Buckingham: Open University Press.

Noddings, N. (2002). *Starting at Home: Caring and Social Policy*. Berkeley, CA: University of California Press.

Norsworthy, K.L. and Gerstein, L.H. (2003). Counselling and Building Communities of Peace: The Interconnections. *International Journal for the Advancement of Counselling* 25, 4, 197–203.

Orbach, S. (1999). *The Impossibility of Sex*. Harmondsworth: Allen Lane.

Oxford Reference Dictionary (1986). London: Guild Publishing.

Page, S. (1999). *The Shadow and the Counsellor*. London: Routledge.

Palmer Barnes, F. and Murdin, L. (eds) (2001). *Values and Ethics in the Practice of Psychotherapy and Counselling*. Buckingham: Open University Press.

Parker, R.S. (1991). The Search for a Relational Ethic of Care. *Advances in Nursing Sciences* 13, 1, 31–40.

Parker, S. (1976). The Precultural Basis of the Incest Taboo: Toward a Biosocial Theory. *American Anthropologist* 78, 2, 285–305.

Parker, W.M. and Schwartz, R.C. (2002). On the Experience of Shame in Multicultural Counselling: Implications for White Counsellors-in-Training. *British Journal of Guidance and Counselling* 30, 3, 311–18.

Pearson, B. and Piazza, N. (1997). Classification of Dual Relationships in the Helping Professions. *Counselor Education and Supervision* 37, 2, 89–99.

Pipes, R.B. (1997). Nonsexual Relationships Between Psychotherapists and Their Former Clients: Obligations of Psychologists. *Ethics and Behavior* 7, 1, 27–41.

Pistole, C. (1989). Attachment: Implications for Counselors. *Journal of Counseling and Development* 68, 2, 190–3.

Polkinghorne, D.E. (2004). Narrative Therapy and Postmodernism. In *The Handbook of Narrative and Psychotherapy: Practice, Theory and Research*, eds. Angus, L.E. and McLeod, J., pp. 53–68. Thousand Oaks, CA: Sage.

POPAN (Prevention of Professional Abuse Network) (1999). Breaking the

Silence: Professional Abuse and its Prevention. Annual conference, November, POPAN, London, UK.

Pope, K.S. (1985). Dual Relationships: A Violation of Ethical, Legal and Clinical Standards. *California State Psychologist* 20, 2, 1–3.

Pope, K.S. (1988a). How Clients are Harmed by Sexual Contact with Mental Health Professionals: The Syndrome and its Prevalence. *Journal of Counseling and Development* 67, 4, 222–6.

Pope, K.S. (1988b). Dual Relationships: A Source of Ethical, Legal, and Clinical Problems. *Independent Practitioner* 8, 1, 17–25.

Pope, K.S. (1990). Therapist–Patient Sexual Contact: Clinical, Legal, and Ethical Implications. In *The Encyclopedia Handbook of Private Practice*, ed. Margenau E.A., pp. 687–96. New York: Gardner Press.

Pope, K.S. (1991). Dual Relationships in Psychotherapy. *Ethics & Behavior* 1, 1, 21–34.

Pope, K.S. (1994). *Sexual Involvement with Therapists: Patient Assessment, Subsequent Therapy, Forensics*. Washington, DC: American Psychological Association.

Pope, K.S. and Bouhoutsos, J.D. (1986). *Sexual Intimacy between Therapists and Patients*. New York: Praeger.

Pope, K.S. and Feldman-Summers, S. (1992). National Survey of Psychologists' Sexual and Physical Abuse History and their Evaluation of Training and Competence in these Areas. *Professional Psychology: Research and Practice* 23, 5, 353–61.

Pope, K.S., Levenson, H. and Schover, L.R. (1979). Sexual Intimacy in Psychology Training: Results and Implications of a National Survey. *American Psychologist* 34, 8, 682–9.

Pope, K.S. and Tabachnick, B.G. (1993). Therapists' Anger, Hate, Fear and Sexual Feelings: National Survey of Therapists' Responses, Client Characteristics, Critical Events, Formal Complaints and Training. *Professional Psychology: Research and Practice* 24, 2, 142–52.

Pope, K.S., Tabachnick, B.G. and Keith-Spiegel, P. (1987). Ethics of Practice: The Beliefs and Behaviors of Psychologists as Therapists. *American Psychologist* 42, 11, 993–1006.

Pope, K.S. and Vasquez, M.J.T. (1998). *Ethics in Psychotherapy and Counseling* (2nd edn). San Francisco: Jossey-Bass.

Pope, K.S. and Vetter, V.A. (1991). Prior Therapist–Patient Sexual Involvement among Patients Seen by Psychologists. *Psychotherapy* 28, 3, 429–38.

Price, J. (1996). Snakes in the Swamp: Ethical Issues in Qualitative Research. In *Ethics and Process in The Narrative Study of Lives*, ed. Josselson, R., pp. 207–15. Thousand Oaks, CA: Sage.

Proctor, G. (2002). *The Dynamics of Power in Counselling and Psychotherapy: Ethics, Politics and Practice*. Manchester: PCCS.

Purtilo, R. (1999). *Ethical Dimensions in the Health Professions* (3rd edn). Philadelphia: W.B. Saunders Company.

Rappoport, L., Baumgardner, S. and Boone, G. (1999). Postmodern Culture and the Plural Self. In *The Plural Self: Multiplicity in Everyday Life*, ed. Rowan, J. and Cooper, M., pp. 93–106. London: Sage.

Reeves, A., Wheeler, S. and Bowl, R. (2004). Assessing Risk: Confrontation or Avoidance – What is Taught on Counselor Training Courses. *British Journal of Guidance and Counselling* 32, 2, 235–47.

Rennie, D.L. (1994a). Client's Deference in Psychotherapy. *Journal of Counseling Psychology* 41, 4, 427–37.

Rennie, D.L. (1994b). Clients' Accounts of Resistance in Counselling: A Qualitative Analysis. *Canadian Journal of Counselling* 28, 1, 43–57.

Rennie, D.L. (1994c). Storytelling in Psychotherapy: The Client's Subjective Experience. *Psychotherapy* 31, 2, 234–43.

Rennie, D.L. (1998). *Person-Centred Counselling: an Experiential Approach*. London: Sage.

Rennie, D.L. (2000). Aspects of the Client's Conscious Control of the Psychotherapeutic Process. *Journal of Psychotherapy Integration* 10, 2, 151–67.

Rennie, D.L. (2001). Clients as Self-Aware Agents. *Counselling and Psychotherapy Research* 1, 2, 82–9.

Rennie, D.L. and Toukmanian, S.G. (1992). Explanation in Psychotherapy Process Research. In *Psychotherapy Process Research: Paradigmatic and Narrative Approaches*, ed. Toukmanian, S.G. and Rennie, D.L. Newbury Park: Sage.

Robson, M., Cook, P., Hunt, K., Aldred, G. and Robson, D. (2000). Towards Ethical Decision-Making in Counselling Research. *British Journal of Guidance and Counselling* 28, 4, 533–48.

Rogers, C.R. (1980). *A Way of Being*. Boston, MA: Houghton Mifflin.

Rowan, J. (1998). *The Reality Game: A Guide to Humanistic Counselling and Psychotherapy* (2nd edn). London: Routledge.

Rowan, J. and Cooper, M. (eds) (1999). *The Plural Self: Multiplicity in Everyday Life*. London: Sage.

Ruddle, P. (1997). General Assessment Issues. In *Client Assessment*, ed. Palmer, S. and McMahon, G., pp. 6–28. London: Sage.

Russell, J. (1993). *Out of Bounds: Sexual Exploitation in Counselling and Therapy*. London: Sage.

Russell, J. (1999). Professional and Socio-Cultural Aspects of the Counselling Relationship. In *Understanding the Counselling Relationship*, ed. Feltham, C., pp. 183–99. London: Sage.

Sands, A. (2000). Falling for Therapy. *Counselling: The Monthly Professional Journal for Counsellors and Psychotherapists* 11, 10, 614–16.

Sands, A. (2002). Psychotherapy from a Client's Point of View. *BPS Psychotherapy Section Newsletter*. No. 32, June 2002, 29–42.

Sarbin, T. (1954). Role Theory. In *Handbook of Social Psychology* (Vol. 1), ed. Lindzey, G., pp. 223–58. Reading, MA: Addison-Wesley.

Sarbin, T. and Allen, V. (1968). Role Theory. In *Handbook of Social Psychology* (Vol. 2), ed. Lindzey, G. Reading, MA: Addison-Wesley.

Schoener, G.R. (1999). Sexual Abuse by Psychotherapists & Other Helping Professionals: Victims, Boundaries and Our Societal Response. Paper presented on 10 July at POPAN (Prevention of Professional Abuse Network). London, England, UK.

Secord, P.F.S. and Backman, C.W.S. (1974). *Social Psychology*. (2nd edn). New York: McGraw-Hill.

Sedgwick, D. (1994). *The Wounded Healer: Countertransference from a Jungian Perspective*. London: Routledge.

Sherwin, S. (2001). Feminist Reflections on the Role of Theories in a Global Bioethics. In *Globalizing Feminist Ethics*, ed. Tong, R., Anderson, G. and Santos, A., pp. 12–26. Boulder, CO: Westview Press.

Sim, J. (1997). *Ethical Decision Making in Therapy Practice*. Oxford, UK: Butterworth-Heinemann.

Simon, R.I. (1992). Treatment Boundary Violations: Clinical, Ethical, and Legal Consideration. *Bulletin of the American Academy of Psychiatry and the Law* 20, 3, 269–88.

Smith, D. and Fitzpatrick, M. (1995). Patient–Therapist Boundary Issues: An Integrating Review of Theory and Research. *Professional Psychology: Research and Practice* 26, 5, 499–506.

Spinelli, E. (2001). *The Mirror and The Hammer: Challenges to Therapeutic Orthodoxies*. London: Continuum.

Spinelli, E. (2003). Embracing the World: Extending the Boundaries of the Therapeutic Relationship. *Psychotherapy Section Newsletter (BPS)*, Vol. 34, 3–14.

Stirzaker, A. (2000). The Taboo which Silences: Is Erotic Transference a Help or a Hindrance in the Counselling Relationship? *Psychodynamic Counselling* 6, 2, 197–213.

Strongman, K.T. (1979). *Psychology for the Paramedical Professions*. London: Croom Helm.

Sue, D.W. and Sue, D. (2003). *Counseling the Culturally Diverse: Theory and Practice* (4th edn). New York: John Wiley & Sons.

Syme, G. (2003). *Dual Relationships in Counselling and Psychotherapy*. London: Sage.

Thomas, G. (1994). A Counsellor First. *Counselling* 5, 1, 44–6.

Thompson, F.E. (2002). Moving from Codes of Ethics to Ethical Relationships for Midwifery Practice. *Nursing Ethics* 9, 5, 522–36.

Thoreson, R.W., Shaughnessy, P. and Frazier, P.A. (1995). Sexual Contact during and after Professional Relationships: Practices and Attitudes of Female Counselors. *Journal of Counseling and Development* 74, 1, 84–9.

Thorne, B. (1987). Beyond the Core Conditions. In *Key Cases in Psychotherapy*, ed. Dryden, W. London: Croom Helm.

Thorne, B.E., Shealy, R.C. and Briggs, S.D. (1993). Sexual Misconduct in Psychotherapy: Reactions to a Consumer-Oriented Brochure. *Professional Psychology* 24, 1, 75–82.

Tong, R., Anderson, G. and Santos, A. (eds) (2001). *Globalizing Feminist Bioethics*. Boulder, CO: Westview Press.

Tudor, K. (1999). I'm OK, You're OK – and They're OK: Therapeutic Relationships in Transactional Analysis. In *Understanding the Counselling Relationship*, ed. Feltham, C., pp. 90–119. London: Sage.

Van Deurzen, E. (1998). *Paradox and Passion in Psychotherapy: An Existential Approach to Therapy and Counselling*. Chichester: Wiley.

Vaspe, A. (2000). Counselling in a Culture of Competence. *Psychodynamic Counselling* 6, 2, 175–96.

Webb, A. (2000). What Makes it Difficult for the Supervisee to Speak? In *Taking Supervision Forward: Enquiries and Trends in Counselling and Psychotherapy*, ed. Lawton, B. and Feltham, C., pp. 60–73. London: Sage.

Webb, S.B. (1997). Training for Maintaining Appropriate Boundaries in Counselling. *British Journal of Guidance and Counselling* 25, 2, 175–89.

Welfel, E.R. (1998). *Ethics in Counselling and Psychotherapy: Standards, Research, and Emerging Issues*. Pacific Grove, CA: Brooks-Cole.

West. W. (2002). Some Ethical Dilemmas in Counselling and Counselling Research. *British Journal of Guidance and Counselling* 30, 3, 262–8.

West, W. (2004). *Spiritual Issues in Therapy – Relating Experience to Practice*. Basingstoke, UK: Palgrave Macmillan.

White, M. and Epston, D. (1992). *Narrative Means to Therapeutic Ends*. New York: Norton.

Widdershoven, G.A.M. and Smits, M. (1996). Ethics and Narratives. In *The Narrative Study of Lives: Ethics and Process in the Narrative Study of Lives*, ed. Josselson, R., pp. 275–88. Thousand Oaks, CA: Sage.

Winslade, J. and Monk, G. (1999) *Narrative Counseling in Schools: Powerful & Brief*. Thousand Oaks, CA: Sage.

Winslade, J. and Monk, G. (2000) *Narrative Mediation: A New Approach to Conflict Resolution*. San Francisco, CA: Jossey-Bass.

Wosket, V. (1999). *The Therapeutic Use of Self: Counselling Practice, Research and Supervision*. London: Routledge.

Wrench, D.F. (1969) *Psychology: A Social Approach*. New York: McGraw-Hill.

Yalom, I.D. (1989). *Love's Executioner and Other Tales of Psychotherapy*. London: Penguin.

Zur, O. (2002a). In Celebration of Dual Relationships: How Prohibition of Nonsexual Dual Relationships Increases the Chance of Exploitation and Harm. In *Dual Relationships and Psychotherapy*, ed. Lazarus, A.A. and Zur, O., pp. 44–54. New York: Springer Publishing Co.

Zur, O. (2002b). Out-of-Office Experience: When Crossing Office Boundaries and Engaging in Dual Relationships are Clinically Beneficial and Ethical Sound. In *Dual Relationships and Psychotherapy*, ed. Lazarus, A.A. and Zur, O., pp. 88–97. New York: Springer Publishing Co.

Zur, O. and Lazarus, A.A. (2002). Six Arguments against Dual Relationships. In *Dual Relationships and Psychotherapy*, ed. Lazarus, A.A. and Zur, O., pp. 3–24. New York: Springer Publishing Co.

Index